From School to Work

Workbook zur Berufsorientierung

Communication

People pass on news and ideas to other people in lots of different ways. Pictures, sounds and words are used to communicate.

1 Communicating in different ways

How many different things in the photo are used to communicate? *Think of more ways to communicate.*

Photo: ______________________________

Your ideas: ______________________________

2 What would you do?

Write what you would do in these situations.

~~tell somebody something quickly~~ tell friends about my trips chat online to my friends relax with my favourite music find out more about a job	... listen to my ... ... use a programme like ... ... check on the ... ... send an e-mail ... ...

1. *If I wanted to tell somebody something quickly, I think I'd send an e-mail or a text message.*
2. *If I wanted to* ______________________________
3. ______________________________
4. ______________________________
5. ______________________________

3 "Mr Watson, I want to see you!"

Read these sentences about the development of the phone. Put them in the right order.

__ He said, "Mr Watson. Come here. I want to see you."

__ In 1927 it was possible to call somebody in London from New York. The phones used radio waves.

__ In 1962 the first communications satellite was sent into space and people could talk all over the world.

__ On March 10, 1876, he spoke through his new invention to his assistant, Thomas Watson, who was in the next room.

1 The first telephone was invented in the 19th century by an American, Alexander Graham Bell.

__ The earliest telephones had one wire, which could only connect two people.

__ However, in the 1990s mobile phones became much cheaper and millions of people could buy them. There are now about 4 billion mobile phones in the world.

__ During the 1970s and 1980s car phones became very popular, but they were expensive.

__ As more and more people wanted phones, they were given their individual phone numbers.

__ Thirty years later telephone cables were laid under the sea from America to Britain.

4 What do you say in English?

Look at these German sentences. What are they in English?

~~Kannst du mich über mein Handy anrufen?~~ • Ich kann mit meinem Handy Videos aufnehmen. • Ich rufe dich heute nachmittag an. • Ich schicke dir eine SMS. • Was hat dein neues Handy gekostet? • Hast du eine neue Handynummer? • Was zahlst du im Monat?

1. Can you ring me on my mobile?
2. ____________
3. ____________
4. ____________
5. ____________
6. ____________
7. ____________

5 Modern technology

Computers have changed our world and the way we work. You need computer skills for lots of jobs.
Say what computer skills you have and what you're good at. You can also say what you're not so good at.

I can ...
I can't ...

I've learned how to ...
I've never ...

I know how to ...
I don't know how to ...

I'm (really) good at ...
I'm not good at ...

use (spreadsheet) software like ...
type quickly / slowly
write documents accurately
build and repair computers
use design programmes like ...
network computers
burn CDs and DVDs
design and create websites
install software like ...

1. I can write documents accurately, but I can't type very quickly.
2. I've learned how to ______________________,
   but I've never ______________________.
3. I'm good at ______________________.
4. ______________________
5. ______________________
6. ______________________
7. ______________________
8. ______________________
9. ______________________

6 Fourth word

Find the fourth word.

1. e-mail – write
   telephone – speak
2. TV – channel
   internet – ______________
3. nothing to do – bored
   lots to do – ______________
4. finish – switch off
   start – ______________
5. taxi – cab
   mobile – ______________
6. pictures – gallery
   books – ______________
7. to meet – meeting
   to advertise – ______________
8. book – title
   newspaper – ______________
9. television – screen
   computer – ______________

7 The multimedia computer

When we talk about computers in German, we often use English words. What are the parts of the computer called? *Write as many names as you can before you look at the vocabulary list at the back of the book.*

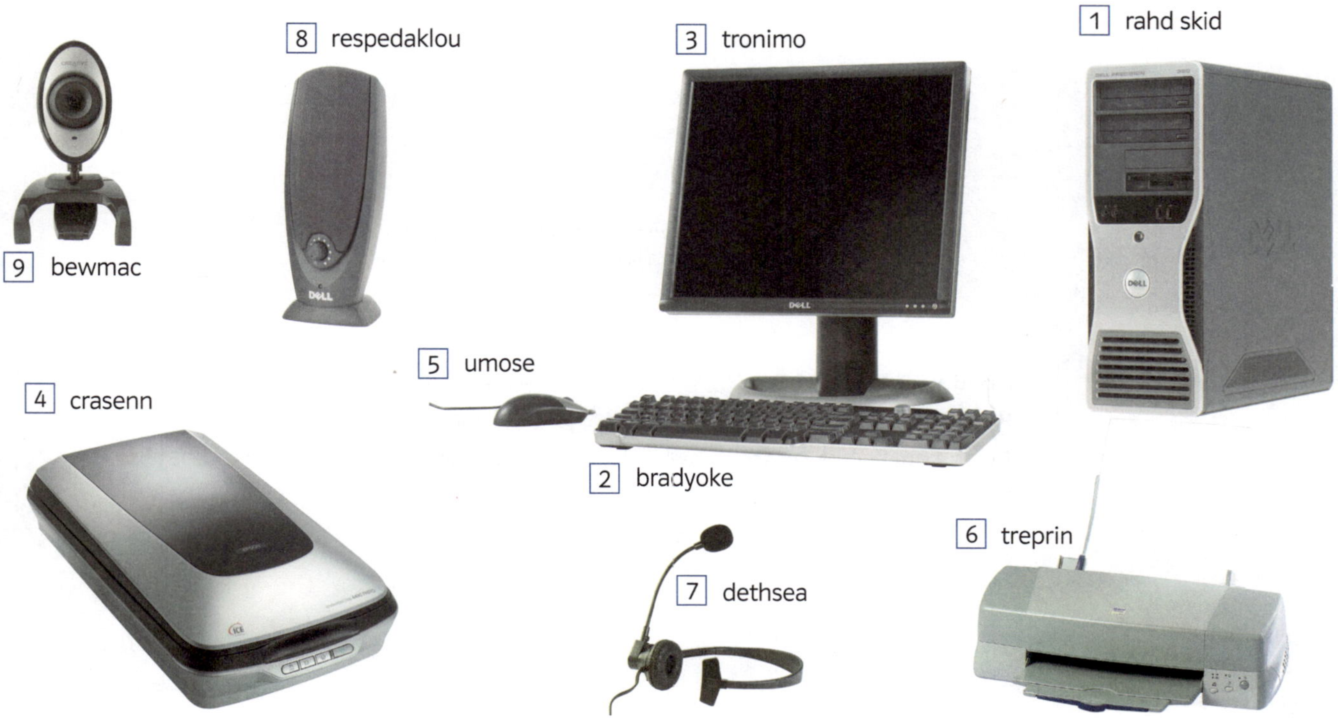

1. ______________ 2. ______________ 3. ______________

4. ______________ 5. ______________ 6. ______________

7. ______________ 8. ______________ 9. ______________

8 Technology gets better all the time

What are the advantages of today's computers? How are they better, faster, more exciting than older computers? *Complete these sentences.*

Today laptops are (1) much lighter than in the past (viel leichter als in der Vergangenheit). (Die leichtesten Laptops) (2) ______________ are only 1 kilo. Some modern laptops are (3) ______________ (so klein wie Bücher). In the past computers were ugly and loud. Modern laptops are (4) ______________ (viel schöner und viel ruhiger) and they have (5) ______________ (viel bessere Bildschirme) with millions of colours.

Today computers play (6) ______________ (eine viel wichtigere Rolle) in offices and in our homes. With wireless Internet it is (7) ______________ (viel einfacher) to sit in the garden and check e-mails. Computer games, which are now (8) ______________ (viel spannender als vorher), often sell millions of copies.

9 Writing to communicate

Mobile phones are a great way to communicate, but people still need to write to each other.
Look at the different texts. Decide what kinds of text they are.

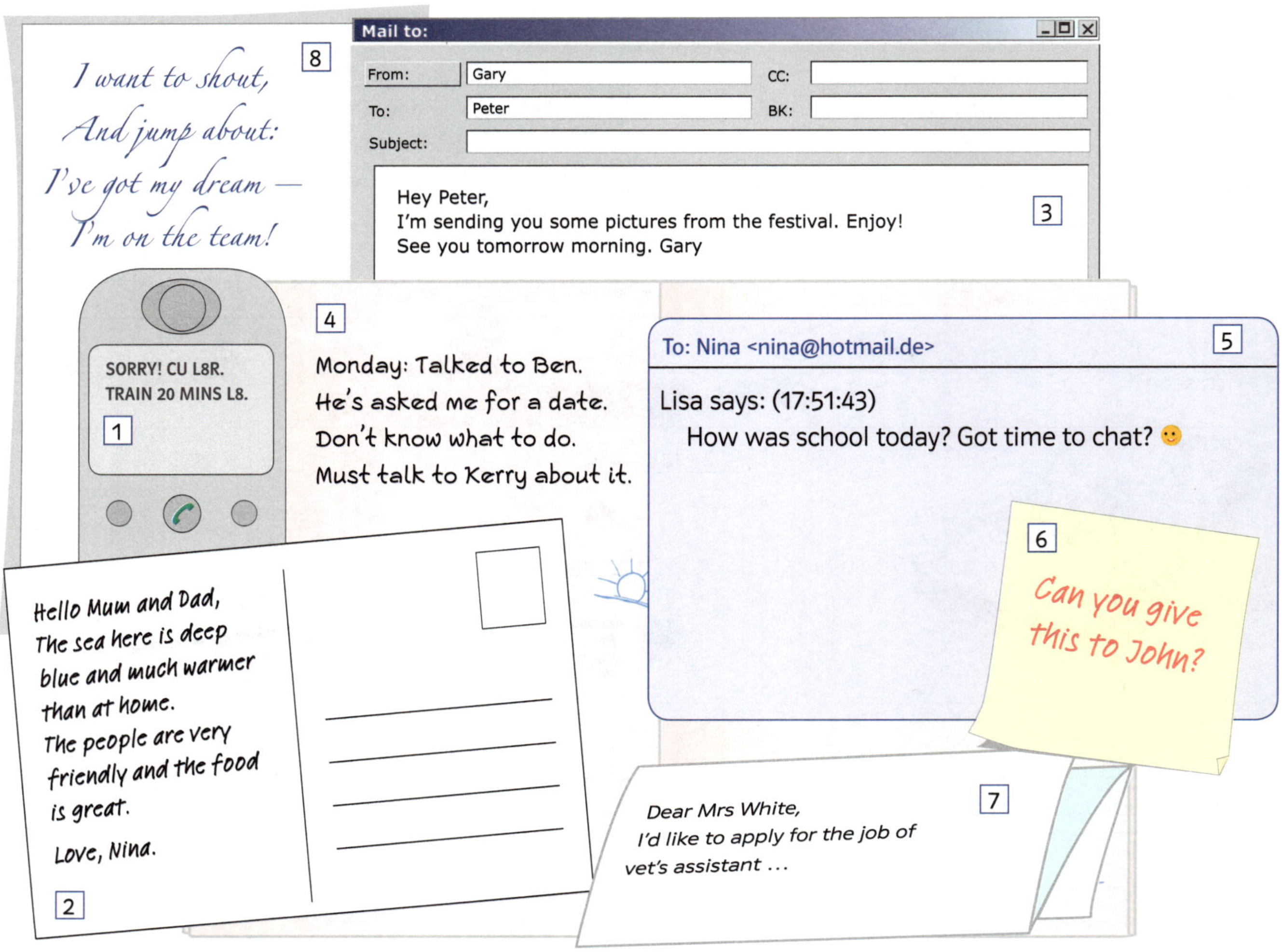

1. *Number one is a text message.*
2. ______
3. ______
4. ______
5. ______
6. ______
7. ______
8. ______

10 Lisa writes lots of texts

What do Lisa's text messages mean? *Write down the full messages.*

GOT GR8 NEWS 4 U • CANT C U 2DAY • THX 4 UR MSG + PIC • TLK 2 U L8R

1. *I've got great news for you.*
2. ______
3. ______
4. ______

11 Writing a text message

Lisa has just got an e-mail. She wants to send the message as a text message to her friend Sonia.
Write the text message.

Hi Lisa
For your information:
The show is tomorrow and costs £20.
Too much, in my opinion. Still want to go?
Tell me as soon as possible. See you.
Carol

N – and • 2moro – tomorrow • imo – in my opinion • asap – as soon as possible • ~~fyi – for your information~~ • 2 – too • wanna – want to • C U – see you

Hi Sonia. Fyi the show is ______

12 Writing notes and letters

When you write a note on paper, you use only the important parts of sentences.
Read this note. Write the message in full sentences.

Hi Robert, I tried to call you earlier. ______

Hi Robert,
Tried to call earlier. Gone to airport. Alex forgot passport! Back at 10. Cook dinner (lasagne in freezer). Call me if problem. Maria

13 Writing postcards

If you go on holiday, some people like getting a postcard from you.
Lisa went to France for a holiday. Write the postcard she sent to her grandparents.

Dear Grandma and Grandpa,
We arrived ______

~~arrive~~/Paris/yesterday
weather/fantastic/sunny
hotel/centre of city
room with three girls
speak French/a disaster
tomorrow/Eiffel Tower

14 Letters are not dead!

Text messages and instant messages are fine with friends. But if you get a job in an office, you will probably have to write letters. If you apply for a job, you'll certainly have to write a letter.

I am sorry about/that ... • Love, • Please find enclosed ... • Could you please send ... • Dear Sir or Madam, • Yours sincerely, • Please accept my apologies about ... • Would you be kind enough to send ... • Write soon. • I look forward to hearing from you. • ~~Hi Ben~~, • I am writing to ask about ... / if ... • Thank you very much (for) ... • Best wishes, • I would like to know if ...

Look at the phrases in the box. Which of these phrases do you use in English letters if you want to ...

1. begin a letter to a friend: Hi Ben,
2. begin a letter to a company: ________
3. get some information: ________
4. thank somebody: ________
5. say you are sorry: ________
6. ask for something: ________
7. send something with a letter: ________
8. finish a letter to a company: ________
9. finish a letter to a friend: ________
10. say you hope to have an answer soon: ________

15 Formal and informal letters

If you write to a friend, you use 'informal language'. If you write to a company, you use 'formal language'. *Look at the phrases in the box. Which are formal? Which are informal? Make lists.*

Yours sincerely, • Thank you very much for your letter. • Can you send me the tickets? • Enjoy! • Keep in touch. • Dear Mr Walker, • ~~What you sent me is rubbish.~~ • Lots of love, • ~~Would you be kind enough to send me a brochure?~~ • Tell me if it's not OK. • I'm afraid I'm not satisfied with the product. • Please contact us if you have any problems. • Hey, it was good to hear from you. • I hope to hear from you soon. • I hope you like the product. • Hello Sam,

informal language	formal language
What you sent me is rubbish.	Would you be kind enough to send me a brochure?

16 Letters to customers

Rebecca Wagner works for Siddharta, a company that makes health products. The company has customers in the USA and Britain. She sometimes has to write to them. *Look at each customer's e-mail and then read the manager's notes for a reply. What would Rebecca write in English?*

Mail to:

From: Robert Evans
CC:
To: mail@siddharta.com
BK:
Subject: health products

Dear Sir or Madam,

I am interested in your products. Do you have a brochure? Can you send it to me electronically? Do you deliver to the USA? How much are delivery costs? How long does it take?

Best wishes,
Robert Evans

- Broschüren ✓
- Als pdf-Datei möglich ✓
- In die USA schicken ✓
- Kosten in EURO. Liste anbei.
- Dauer: ca. 2 Wochen.
- Zurückschicken: kein Problem.
- Wir erstatten alle Kosten.
- Porto übernimmt der Sender.

Mail to:

From: Megan Lowerton
CC:
To: mail@siddharta.com
BK:
Subject: GreenLife – my order

Dear Sir or Madam,
I ordered GreenLife on your website. I paid €48. That was three weeks ago. I haven't received anything yet.
I'm really annoyed about this.
Megan Lowerton

- Es tut uns sehr leid.
- Wir gehen der Sache nach.
- Wenn noch nicht geschickt wurde – dann wird sofort geschickt.
- Wir hoffen, GreenLife gefällt ihr.

Dear Mr Evans,

Dear Mrs Lowerton,

17 Could I speak to Mr White, please?

Alex works in an office. She answers the phone when clients call. *Complete this phone conversation.*

Thank you for calling • ~~How can I help you?~~ • Can I take a message? • Can you call back later? • Who's calling, please? • Just a moment

ALEX: Good morning. This is Ravenswood Technology . My name is Alex. (1) How can I help you?

SAMANTHA: Good morning. Could I speak to Jason White, please?

ALEX: (2) ______

SAMANTHA: Oh, I'm sorry. My name is Samantha Willams. I'm from Solar Media.

ALEX: (3) ______ . I'll see if Mr White is in his office.

SAMANTHA: Thank you.

ALEX: Ms Williams? I'm afraid Mr White is in a meeting at the moment.

SAMANTHA: Oh, I see. When can I speak to him?

ALEX: The meeting will be over in about half an hour. (4) ______

SAMANTHA: OK. I'll phone back at eleven o'clock.

ALEX: (5) ______

SAMANTHA: Yes, please. Tell him that we haven't received the equipment we ordered. I'd like to know if you have sent it.

ALEX: I'll be happy to give him your message. (6) ______

SAMANTHA: Thank you. Goodbye.

18 Phone phrases

Robert has just phoned his friend, Lewis Best. Lewis's mother answers the phone. *Use the sentences in the box to complete the phone conversation. Be careful! There are more sentences than you need.*

Have you got a mobile? • Exeter 318795. Caroline Best speaking • Good idea. I'll tell him you called, Robert. • Sorry, Robert. Lewis is out. • Yes, who is it? • I'm sorry, I don't. Can I take a message?

MRS BEST: ______

ROBERT: Hi, it's Robert here. Is Lewis at home?

MRS BEST: ______

ROBERT: Oh, do you know when he will be home?

MRS BEST: ______

ROBERT: No, it's fine. I'll call him on his mobile.

MRS BEST: ______

ROBERT: Thanks. Goodbye.

19 First or second?

A *Look at these words. Is the stress on the first or the second syllable? Mark the syllable which is stressed.*

con|tact	pre|fer	sur|vey	ad|vert
a|ddress	re|sults	mo|bile	pro|gramme
leaf|let	en|joy	ex|plain	in|vent

B *Complete these sentences with words from the list above.*

1. I have to ______________________ to my mother how her new mobile phone works.
2. The tourist information office has a ______________________ with all the sights of our town.
3. Did you ______________________ the party last night? Was it good?
4. Why can't we ______________________ a car that doesn't need petrol but runs on water?
5. The ______________________ shows that more young people watch Big Brother than news reports.
6. I don't really like potatoes. I'd ______________________ a salad with my meal. Is that OK?

20 Word groups

Look at the four groups. Find at least five words for each group. Some words can go into more than one group.

advert • article • caller • cartoons • channel • commercial • documentary • DVD • headline • Internet • interview • journalist • keyboard • mobile • monitor • Pay As You Go • phone number • programme • reporter • ring tone • software • text message • username • webcam •

computer	**telephone**
______________________	______________________
______________________	______________________
______________________	______________________
______________________	______________________
______________________	______________________

newspaper	**television**
______________________	______________________
______________________	______________________
______________________	______________________
______________________	______________________
______________________	______________________

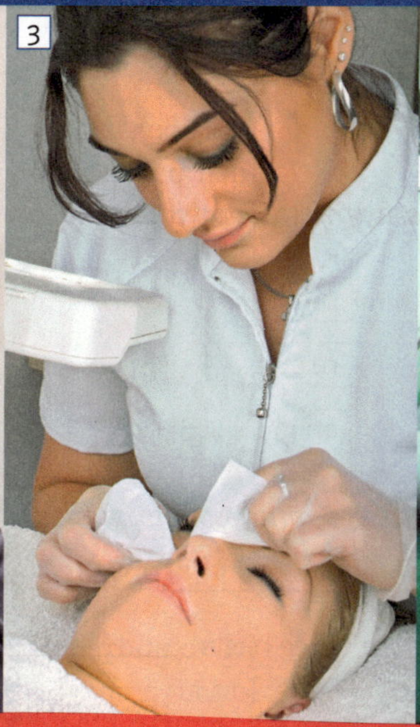

Career plans

We all have different ideas about where we'd like to work and what we'd like to do. We all have our own idea of 'the perfect job'.

1 The perfect job

electrician • cook • truck driver • hairdresser • beauty therapist • soldier • secretary • police officer • carer • plumber • sales assistant • builder • photographer • painter and decorator • pilot • lifeguard • mechanic • nurse • hotel receptionist • computer engineer • journalist

A *Look at the list of jobs. Look at the photos. What jobs are the people doing?*

1. ____________ 2. ____________ 3. ____________ 4. ____________

B People have different opinions about some jobs. *Choose jobs from the list above and write sentences.*

~~repair things that are broken~~ • work long hard hours • fly to different countries • look after sick people • cars always break down • find and arrest criminals

1. practical: *A computer engineer is a practical job because you repair things that are broken.*
2. exciting: ____________
3. stressful: ____________
4. valuable: ____________
5. useful: ____________
6. dangerous: ____________

2 What are our jobs?

Find two jobs for each description.

~~actor~~ • caretaker • ~~dancer~~ • doctor • driver • electrician • farmer • goalkeeper • headteacher • mechanic • nurse • plumber • receptionist • tennis player • vet's assistant • waiter

1. We work in a theatre. dancer, actor
2. We work with animals. ______
3. We both have jobs in a school. ______
4. We work in a hotel. ______
5. We work in a hospital. ______
6. Our jobs have to do with cars and lorries. ______
7. Our work has to do with sports. ______
8. People need us when they build or repair a house. ______

3 Gina Schmidt – hotel receptionist in Stuttgart

Read what Gina says about her job. How would you describe her daily routine in English?

„Ich arbeite als Rezeptionistin in einem großen internationalen Hotel. Ich fange normalerweise um sechs Uhr an, bevor die Gäste zum Frühstück gehen. Ich begrüsse die neuen Gäste, und ich nehme Anrufe entgegen. Ich rede oft mit den Gästen und helfe ihnen, wenn sie Fragen haben.
Ich habe immer nur eine halbe Stunde Mittagspause und esse im Hotel. Normalerweise gehe ich um halb vier nach Hause. Aber manchmal verspätet sich meine Kollegin, dann muss ich etwas länger bleiben."

Gina works as a receptionist in a large international hotel. She usually ______

4 I'm good at that!

You'll be happier in your job if you can do something you are good at, or if you can do some of the things you like doing. *Write sentences to describe yourself. Say what you could do, and what you wouldn't like to do. Look at the example. Be careful! Use the correct form of the verb.*

I'm ...	**I can ...**	**I enjoy/like ...**	**I can imagine ...**
creative	organise things	be my own boss	work as a plumber
practical	type well	be outdoors	work as a vet's assistant
organised	work well under pressure	be with other people	work for a newspaper
outgoing		travel and see new places	work for a garden centre
caring			work for a hotel
committed			work for a construction company
a born leader			work in a hospital
a good team player			work in a garage
good with my hands			

1. *I'm a practical person. I enjoy being outdoors. I can imagine working for a garden centre.*
2. I'm ____________________.
3. I'm not very __________. I don't __________.
   I don't think I would like to __________.
4. ____________________

5 Strange jobs

Some people want to do jobs that are really different. *Read about the ring tone recorder. Now choose one of these jobs. Describe what this person must do.*

Ring tone recorder
This is a new type of profession. These are the people who write and record those annoying little tunes that people hate when a mobile rings on trains and in buses. After all, somebody has to do it. Ring tones are very popular, so if you want to be successful you have to think of a melody that people will want.

Chewing gum buster

Dog detective

6 Derek's job

Complete these sentences about Derek, who works in a leisure centre. Be careful with tenses.

1. Derek works______ (work) as a lifeguard in a leisure centre.
2. He ______ (start) two months ago.
3. He usually ______ (start) at six in the morning and ______ (finish) at two in the afternoon.
4. Next week he ______ (start) in the afternoon. He ______ (work) till 10 in the evening.
5. He really enjoys ______ (work) in the sports centre, but there are some jobs that he ______ (not like).
6. He hates ______ (clean) the pool and the changing rooms.
7. Yesterday he ______ (save) a young boy who ______ (fall) into the pool.
8. Derek ______ (earn) £5.50 an hour. He ______ (get) £6.50 if he ______ (work) on Sunday.

7 'Fifteen' – a special restaurant

Jamie Oliver is a popular TV cook. In 2002 Jamie Oliver opened a restaurant in London. He called it 'Fifteen'. He gave it this name because he trained 15 unemployed teenagers to become cooks. *Complete the sentences.*

TIPP

Das Passiv sagt aus, was mit einer Person, einem Tier oder einem Gegenstand gemacht wird.

Das Passiv in der Gegenwart:
is/are + *dritte Verbform*
Das Passiv in der Vergangenheit:
was/were + *dritte Verbform*

The restaurant 'Fifteen' **was opened** in London in 2002.

1. 'Fifteen' was opened______ in London in 2002.
2. The restaurant ______ by Jamie Oliver himself.
3. 15 teenagers, who had no jobs, ______ work in the restaurant.
4. They ______ by Jamie Oliver to become cooks in his restaurant.
5. Many had never cooked before, but they ______ to cook five star meals.
6. At the end of the training reporters and famous people ______ to the restaurant.
7. All the meals ______ by the fifteen teenagers.
8. A film ______ about the restautant and it ______ on television.
9. 'Fifteen' became so popular that another restaurant ______ in Cornwall in 2006.
10. Through Jamie Oliver's work a lot of teenagers who had no hope ______ a new chance.

~~open~~
plan
give
train
teach
invite
cook
make; show
build
offer

8 Talking about career plans

Some teenagers already know exactly what job they want after school. Others know what kind of job they would like, but they don't know exactly which job. They need more information.

A *Read about Kate, Mark and Jennifer. Answer the questions.*

KATE: "I've always liked fashion. I like looking at new styles and I know what looks good on my friends. When I leave school, I'll start training to become a hairdresser at Amanda Marsden – one of the best hairdressers in town. I used to work there part-time, so I already have lots of experience. The perfect job for me would be a hairdresser for film stars. But there are none in Bridgend."

GARDENER

JENNIFER: " I'm going to be a mechanic when I leave school. My father is a mechanic and I've worked with him since I was very young. He's taught me a lot. I'll work in my father's garage first. But soon I want to start my own company with my best friend. Our dream is to custom-build motorbikes. I'm sure we'll be popular with our friends when their cars break down."

HAIRDRESSER

MARK: "My dream was to be a pilot but I've found out that my eyes are not good enough. I'm really disappointed and I don't know what I want to do now. Perhaps I'll become a gardener. I love being outside, I love nature and I'm good at working with my hands. My parents say I should become a plumber– there's always enough work, and it's well-paid. I think I need some more advice before I decide."

MECHANIC

1. Kate wants to be a hairdresser because …
   a) she knows Amanda Marsden.
   b) she knows what looks good on people.
   c) she can't get a job as a fashion designer.
2. Kate has …
   a) never worked for a hairdresser before.
   b) has given haircuts to film stars.
   c) worked for a hairdresser part-time.
3. Mark can't be a pilot because …
   a) he is colour blind.
   b) his eyes are not good enough.
   c) his parents are disappointed in him.
4. Mark's parents think he ought to work as …
   a) a plumber.
   b) a gardener.
   c) a pilot.
5. Jennifer has learned a lot from working with …
   a) her father.
   b) her father's colleagues.
   c) her friends.
6. She will work for her father, but later she wants to …
   a) have her own company with her friend.
   b) work alone in her father's garage.
   c) only repair her friends' cars.

B What are you going to do when you leave school? *Write at least three full sentences about yourself.*

9 Advice for Maria

Maria is unsure what the best job would be. She can ask lots of people about jobs and careers, but not all the opinions will be helpful. What are the advantages and disadvantages for Maria if she asks the following people for advice? *What do you think? Use the ideas in the box to write your answers.*

Friends	**Careers advisor**	**Parents or relatives**
easier to talk to them ☺	skills and abilities	experience of working life
personality and interests ☺	what employers are looking for	the jobs with the most money
no real work experience ☹	find the best job	trends in the job market
old enough to give advice ☹	know the best jobs that are available	(not) know what's really best

1. If she asks her friends, it'll be easier to talk to them. They'll know her personality and interests.
   However, they won't ______
   And unfortnately, they won't ______
2. If she talks to ______
   ______
   ______
   ______
3. ______
   ______
   ______
   ______

10 A waiter's life is not an easy life

Here are some English jokes about waiters. *Match the parts to make the jokes.*

A	B	C	D
It's the hot water that kills them.	**Don't worry, sir. It isn't hot.**	**That's right, madam. Two chips and a pea.**	**I'm afraid you can't, madam. He's gone out to lunch.**

1. Waiter, waiter! Do you call this a three-course meal?
2. Waiter, waiter! There is a dead fly in my soup!
3. Waiter, waiter! I want to complain! I want to speak to the cook!
4. Waiter, waiter! You have your finger in my soup!

1. 1 goes with C 2. ______
3. ______ 4. ______

11 Nick's interview with a careers advisor

What did Nick say when he talked to his advisor, Mrs Clark?

Nick hat eine Idee. Er hofft, dass Mrs Clark ihm helfen kann.	MRS CLARK: Good morning, Nick. So, have you decided about next year? NICK: I've had an idea. I hope ____________________ MRS CLARK: Great. Well, tell me about it, Nick.
Nick würde gern für einen Radiosender arbeiten. Er möchte gern DJ oder Moderator sein.	NICK: ____________________ ____________________ MRS CLARK: That's interesting. Is there a special reason why you chose this job?
Er kennt sich mit Musik gut aus und er hat eine gute Stimme.	NICK: ____________________ ____________________ MRS CLARK: Have you had any experience with this kind of work?
Nick bejaht dies. Seine Freunde haben eine Band. Nick macht Computeraufnahmen ihrer Musik und verkauft sie online.	NICK: ____________________ ____________________ MRS CLARK: Excellent. Why don't you contact the local radio station? Tell them what you can do. They will be very interested.
Nick fragt, ob Frau Clark wisse, wo er eine Ausbildung oder ein Praktikum machen kann.	NICK: ____________________ ____________________ MRS CLARK: At RM1 Radio you can do an apprenticeship to be a sound engineer.
Nick findet die Idee gut. Er wird den Sender anrufen und fragen, ob sie ihm weiterhelfen könnten.	NICK: ____________________ ____________________ MRS CLARK: Well, good luck. I hope you can find a job you enjoy.
Nick bedankt sich und verabschiedet sich.	NICK: ____________________

12 Missing words

Look at the words in the box. Find the right words to complete these sentences.

colleagues • salary • employees • wages • employer • minimum wage • tax • unemployed

1. When you work, you get money every month. This is called your ______________ or your ______________.
2. If you don't have a job, you are ____________________ .
3. When you earn money, you must pay some of this to the government. This is called ____________________ .
4. The person or company that gives you a job and pays you is your ____________________ .
5. If you work, you cannot earn less than a certain amount of money. This called the ____________________ .
6. The people you work with are called your ____________________ .
7. The people who work for a company or a firm are called ____________________.

13 Right person – right job

A What sort of person are the employers looking for in these adverts? *Highlight the part of the advert which tells you what the person should be like (qualities), or what the person should be good at (skills).*

City park gardener
We are looking for someone to help us to keep the park clean and green. No experience needed. You must be willing to work outdoors and use heavy garden tools. Ideal for someone who likes plants and wants to do physical work. Flexible hours, minimum wage.
Call: 01803 200200

Welcome on board!
Friendly, energetic young people wanted for work as stewards and stewardesses on cross-channel ferries. Candidates should have experience with customers. Must be willing to work long hours. Good pay and bonuses.
Contact Sally at: seacross@channelcrossers.co.uk

Secretary for computer software company
Full-time, good pay.
Good computer skills necessary.
Experience with standard office software a must.
Must have a friendly personality.
E-mail CV to: info@topsoftware.co.uk

WAITER/WAITRESS REQUIRED.
Busy restaurant in town centre needs hard-working waiter/waitress. Full-time or part-time.
Evening and weekend shifts only.
Must be friendly and able to work under pressure.
Salary meets minimum wage. Big tips. Great team.
Call: 01392 7742211

B *Find the answers for each question.*

1. For which two jobs is experience needed? *Experience is needed for the secretary and steward/stewardess.*
2. You can earn extra money in which two jobs? *You can earn* ______
3. Which quality must a secretary have? ______
4. Which two jobs offer the minimum wage? ______
5. In which two jobs will you work mostly with customers? ______
6. Which two jobs could have the most physical work? ______

C In your opinion, what are the advantages and disadvantages of each job?
Copy this grid into your exercise book and write your ideas. Compare your answers with your friends.

	advantages	disadvantages
city park gardener	*– no experience necessary*	*– You have to do a lot of physical work.*
steward/stewardess		
secretary		
waiter/waitress		

14 Working abroad

After school Katrin would like to go abroad for a few months before she starts a college course. She found some information on a website for young people who are interested in working abroad. Here are two interesting jobs.

Do YOU want to volunteer around the world?
We need your help! We offer 3- or 6-month projects in different countries:
- Help to build a school in Bolivia.
- Plant trees in India.
- Save water in Sudan.

Food and accommodation are free.
Volunteers pay for flights and bring their own pocket money.
Check out our website: www.myworldvolunteer.org

American dream? Be an au pair in the USA!
Come and live with an American family and look after the kids.
Take them to the movies; Help with their homework; Have fun!
Accommodation, flights and pocket money are all included.
Be a big brother! Male au pairs especially welcome!
This could be the best summer of your life!
Contact: rupert@usaupairing.co.org

A *In your exercise book write a summary in German for each job advert. Describe what you can do. Say what the conditions are and how you apply.*

B *Read the adverts again. Correct this information.*

1. Volunteers have to do 3 or 6 projects.

___

2. Volunteers who agree to work for 6 months get a salary.

___

3. Volunteers can only work in India.

___

4. Volunteers have to bring a tent.

___

5. The American au pair company only takes boys.

___

6. If you want to work as an au pair, you must work all year.

___

7. Au pairs must pay for their own flights to the USA and they get a good salary.

___

8. Au pairs only look after the children.

___

C *In your exercise book write an e-mail to apply for one of the jobs. Tell the organisation who you are, how old you are and why you are writing. Write about any relevant experience you have. Ask a question about the job.*

15 A crossword

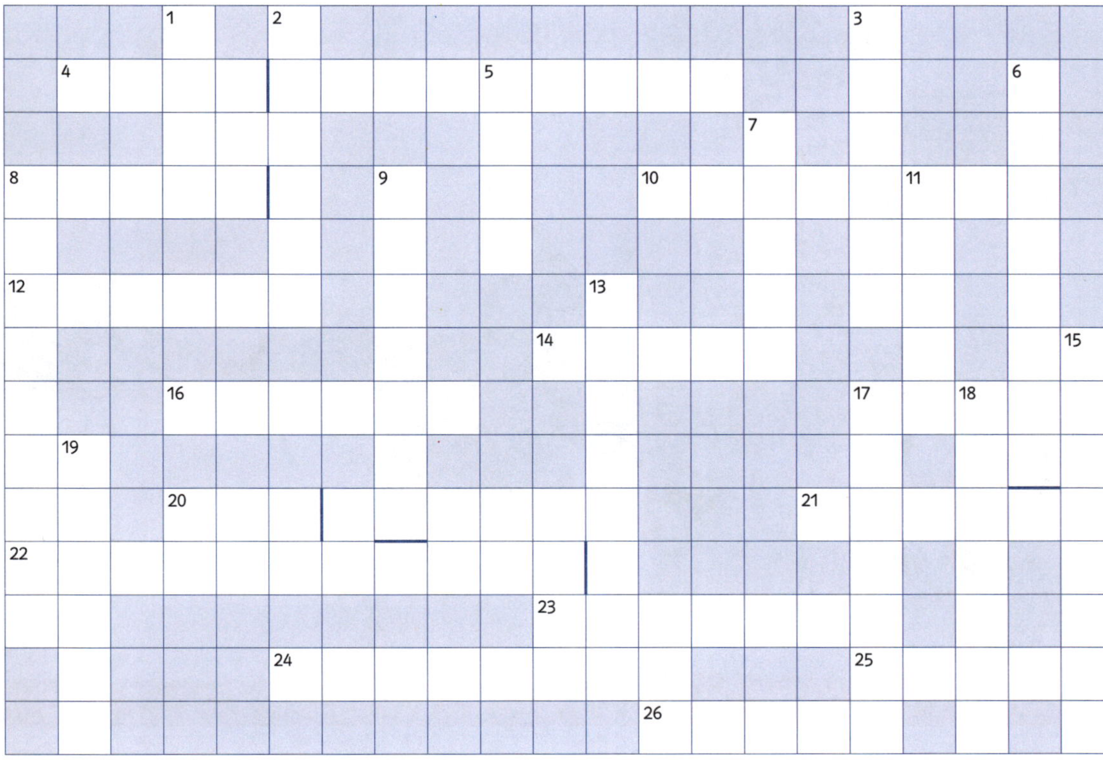

Across

4. Someone who sells things in a shop.
8. He or she looks after people in hospital.
10. If you can decide when you work, your hours are … .
12. Someone who works in restaurant.
14. If you work as a baker, you have to get up very … .
16. This person lives with a family in the USA and looks after the children.
20. A place where you can find out about jobs and careers.
21. I'd like a job where I can … and see foreign countries.
22. This person installs electricity in the house.
23. The two days at the end of the week.
24. Inside a computer – not hardware, but … .
25. If you don't work in a team, you usually work … .
26. I can't carry these boxes, they are too … .

Down

1. The person who tells you what to do is your … .
2. All the different jobs you have in your working life.
3. This is the place where a secretary works.
5. If someone is very ill, he or she is a … person.
6. If you have lots of ideas for ways to do things, you are a … person.
7. A boat that takes you from one side of the water to another.
8. One place where you can find job adverts.
9. The opposite of inside.
11. If you do a job well, your firm might give you a … .
13. Someone who looks after trees and plants in a garden or park.
15. The person who you work for is your … .
17. When you work you usually have five of these days in one week.
18. The person who answers your questions and gives you advice about jobs.
19. When you speak to people in a respectful, friendly way, you are … .

Applications and interviews

When you are looking for a job you want to make a good impression on an employer. It's a good idea to learn the dos and don'ts about job applications and job interviews.

1 Applying for a job

Look at the photos. Describe what happened when Jason looked for a job. Use the phrases in the box. Use the verbs in the correct form.

start on Monday • write a letter of application • offer him a job as a trainee cook • sound perfect • phone the restaurant • read the job adverts • invite him for an interview • ~~become a cook~~ • make a good impression

1. When Jason finished school, he decided that he wanted to ___become a cook___ in a restaurant.
2. He ________________ in all the newspapers.
3. He found one interesting advert that ________________ .
4. He ________________ to ask for more information.
5. After that he ________________ and sent it to the manager with his CV.
6. One week later the manager of the restaurant ________________ .
7. He must have ________________ because the manager wrote to him the next day.
8. He ________________ and said Jason could ________________ .

2 Writing a CV

When you apply for a job, your future employer will ask for a CV. This is information about you and your life. It's a good idea to update your CV regularly. *Look at Jason's CV, then answer the questions.*

Personal details • name • address with postcode • e-mail address • telephone number • nationality • date of birth	 **Jason Williams** 14 King's Road, Bristol, BS3 6YJ, United Kingdom jdwilliams@firstmail.com 0117 435789 British 28th June 1992
Summary Describe yourself. Write a brief summary of your skills and interests.	I am a motivated and reliable person. I have a good sense of humour and most of my friends say I am a friendly person. I finish school in July and I hope to leave with good qualifications. I am keen on sport: I play football (member of a club) and basketball.
Education Say which schools you have attended. Give the dates. Say what qualifications you have.	**2002–2008:** Bristol North City Academy (GCSE 2008: 2 As, 4 Bs, 4 Cs) **1996–2002:** Hill Road Primary School
Work experience Give details of any work experience. Give exact dates and say what you did.	**September 2008:** Two weeks work experience at the Green Elephant Restaurant. I worked in the kitchen. **since 2007:** Saturday job as a waiter in the restaurant in Hoopers department store.
Additional skills and interests • sporting achievements • interests and hobbies • language skills • computer skills	I play football regularly for Bristol Tigers Football Club. I have played in our school football team and I play basketball for our school. I also help with my father's boat rental company. I sometimes take people on fishing trips. My mother tongue is English and I have learned French at school. I can use standard office software. I can also use Linux.

Find the English equivalents for these German words and phrases.

1. motiviert und zuverlässig ____________________
2. Geburtsdatum ____________________
3. sportliche Leistungen ____________________
4. Anschrift und Postleitzahl ____________________
5. Computerkenntnisse ____________________
6. Berufspraktikum ____________________
7. Staatsangehörigkeit ____________________
8. eine kurze Zusammenfassung ____________________
9. Interessen und Hobbies ____________________
10. gute Qualifikationen ____________________
11. Sprachkenntnisse ____________________
12. als Kellner/Kellnerin ____________________

3 Writing your own CV

Write a CV for yourself.

Personal details

Summary

Education

Work experience

Additional skills and interests

4 Looking for a job

Jupiter Electronics wants to employ new people. *Read the information and answer the questions.*

Jupiter Electronics

HOME about us | products | contact us | support

Jupiter Electronics is one of the UK's leading electronics companies.
The company's headquarters are in Bristol.
We have over 1000 stores in the UK.
Jupiter Electronics is expanding to other European countries. We plan to open the first stores in Germany this year.
We sell a wide range of consumer electronic products and electrical household appliances, from TVs and home cinemas to washing machines and fridges.

Welcome to Jupiter Electronics!

JOBS
Jupiter Electronics is looking for people to train as sales personnel in its main branch in Bristol.
Salary depends on experience and qualifications.
We are looking for flexible, reliable people who are prepared to work hard.
Candidates must have basic computer skills and good spoken and written English.
For more information, please contact emma.davidson@jup-uk.com, or phone 0711 989564.
Candidates should send their CV and a cover letter to Emma Davidson, Jupiter Electronics.

OPENING HOURS
Monday to Friday: 9am – 6.30pm
Saturday: 10am – 5pm

We can guarantee the cheapest prices for our customers.

1. Jupiter Electronics is looking for …
   a) young people to do work experience.
   b) people who want to train as sales personnel.
   c) people who want to learn basic computer skills.

2. Candidates should …
   a) be flexible and reliable and work hard.
   b) have experience.
   c) have lots of qualifications.

3. You can buy these products in Jupiter stores …
   a) wardrobes, cupboards, beds.
   b) music, books, magazines.
   c) radios, TVs, computers.

4. Jupiter Electronics has …
   a) one store in Germany.
   b) over 1000 stores in the UK.
   c) over 1000 stores in the UK and Europe.

5 Find the words

Find the words and phrases in the text that have these meanings.

1. men and women who sell things in a department store ___sales personnel___
2. the money you earn for working ______
3. people who apply for a job ______
4. the main or central office of a company ______
5. to grow means to ______
6. another word for shop ______
7. to make a promise that the price is the cheapest ______
8. people who come to a shop to buy something ______
9. TVs, MP3 players, digital cameras, DVD players ______
10. a document or diploma that says how well you can do something ______

6 Phoning about a job

Julia Nicholls from Bristol will leave school soon. She has seen that Jupiter Electronics are looking for sales personnel. She decides to phone and ask if they still have any vacancies. Before she phones, she remembers the telephone tips which her careers advisor gave her.

A *Match the parts of the sentences to make the tips.*

1. It's a good idea to write down →	the person you are talking to.
2. Remember the name of	so talk clearly and politely.
3. Explain briefly	make notes during the phone call.
4. It's important to make a good impression,	→ all your questions before you call the company.
5. You don't want to forget important information, so	thank the person and say goodbye.
6. At the end of the phone call don't forget to	why you are phoning and what you want to know.

B *In your exercise book write a summary of the tips in German.*

7 Do you have any vacancies?

What did Julia say when she phoned Jupiter Electronics? Use the ideas in the box for help.

vacancies at the moment? • experience necessary? • qualifications? • apply? • start? • address? • say 'Thank you'

MRS DAVIDSON: Good morning. This is Jupiter Electronics.
My name is Emma Davidson. How can I help you?

JULIA: Good morning. My name is Julia Nicholls.
(1) I'd like to know if ______________________________ .

MRS DAVIDSON: Yes, we do. We are still looking for sales personnel in our stores in Bristol.

JULIA: I see. (2) ______________________________?

MRS DAVIDSON: No, it isn't necessary. We will give you the right training.

JULIA: I see. (3) ______________________________?

MRS DAVIDSON: You should have good grades in English.

JULIA: That's fine. I've got an A in English. (4) How ______________________________?

MRS DAVIDSON: Write a letter of application and send a CV to me.

JULIA: Ok, I'll do that today. (5) When ______________________________?

MRS DAVIDSON: You could start immediately. We are looking for people now.

JULIA: Excellent. (6) ______________________________?

MRS DAVIDSON: It's Bond House, 11-14 Walker Road, Bristol BS1 2CF. You could also send it in an e-mail.

JULIA: (7) ______________________________

MRS DAVIDSON: Goodbye.

8 Julia's letter of application

After her phone call, Julia wrote a letter of application.

17 Kings Road
Bristol BS12 9TG

Mrs Emma Davidson
Human Resources Department
JUPITER ELECTRONICS
Bond House
11–14 Walker Road
Bristol BS1 2CF

20th June 20…

Dear Mrs Davidson,

Trainee sales personnel

I am writing to apply for the job of trainee salesperson.
I finish school in July this year and I expect to leave with good qualifications.
Please find enclosed my current CV.
For the last year I have worked on Saturdays as a sales assistant in a department store. I am a hard worker and I enjoy working with customers.
I would be very glad to have the opportunity to work for your company.
I am available for an interview at any time.
I look forward to hearing from you.

Yours sincerely,

J. Nicholls
Julia Nicholls

Enclosed: CV

A *What did Julia write in English?*

1. Mit diesem Schreiben bewerbe ich mich für ______
2. In der Anlage finden Sie ______
3. Ich habe samstags als Verkäuferin gearbeitet. ______
4. Sehr geehrte Frau Davidson ______
5. Ich freue mich auf Ihre Antwort. ______
6. Mit freundlichen Grüßen ______

B *Look at this advert. In your exercise book write a letter of application to TeenFashion.*

TeenFashion Magazine ***The number one choice for cool girls.***
We need a full-time advertising assistant.
Is fashion your passion? Are you creative? Do you know what is cool?
Some work experience needed. Must be prepared to work hard.
Send a letter and CV to sam@teenfashion.net

9 Who are you?

Work experience is a good way to find out if you like a job or a company. But sometimes it is not a happy experience. *Read about Alex Fenton's work experience. Use the words in the box to complete his story.*

advertising department • completely forgotten • didn't tell us • had lost my job • motorbike holiday • on holiday • ~~television company~~ • the manager • the receptionist • very busy • very helpful • Who are you?

I worked at Blue Hat Media for two weeks.

I was really excited because Blue Hat Media is a big (1) television company ________.

I am interested in art, so they said I could work in the (2) ________.

When I arrived on Monday morning, (3) ________ showed me where the department was. She didn't have much time because she was (4) ________, so she left me outside the door. I went into the room and looked for Mr Perkins. He was (5) ________ of the department and my new boss, so he should tell me what to do.

"Hello, I am Alex," I said. "Is Mr Perkins here? Today is my first day of work experience."

The lady who was sitting near the door smiled. "Really? Mr Perkins is (6) ________."

He will be back in two weeks. We know nothing about you. He (7) ________ that you were coming." What a first day! But after that, everyone in the office was (8) ________.

They gave me lots of small jobs to do.

On my last day, Mr Perkins came into the office. He told us about his fantastic (9) ________.

When he had finished, he looked at me and asked, (10) "________"

Everyone laughed and they told him about me. He had (11) ________ about me. He was very sorry. Then he said, "For a moment, I thought I (12) ________ and you were the new manager!"

10 Opposites

Write the opposite of the part of the sentence.

1. I enjoy working on <u>weekdays</u>. weekends
2. I <u>left</u> college in July. ________
3. I'd like to work <u>outdoors</u>. ________
4. I was <u>nervous</u> during the interview. ________
5. I'd like to work <u>in a team</u>. ________
6. I <u>forgot</u> to send the letter to Blue Hat Media. ________

11 I wouldn't employ you!

Alex and his father often have different ideas about work and jobs.
Read this conversation between Alex and his father. Use the words in the box to make sentences.

FATHER: Your mother tells me you are finally looking for a job. It's about time!
ALEX: That's right. *I've applied for a job as a photographer.* ______.

apply/job/ photographer

FATHER: What! There are a million photographers. What are you thinking of?
ALEX: I like the idea. I think I ______.

enjoy/work/ photographer

FATHER: Why is that?
ALEX: I'm sure I ______.

great fun/ famous people

FATHER: You should become a plumber. That's what I think. You'll always have work.
I'm ______.

good at/take/ photographs

FATHER: Really? I wouldn't employ you. You're too lazy.
ALEX: ______
I'll be really motivated.

not lazy/when/ start/earn money

FATHER: Motivated? When was the last time you went to football training? You should start doing more sport. Employers will be impressed if you have sports in your CV.
ALEX: They'll ______
______.

more impressed/ read/ work experience

FATHER: Oh, that! You spent two weeks in an office and nobody knew why you were there!
ALEX: That was a mistake. ______
______

manager/forgot/ tell the others/on holiday

FATHER: When I was your age, we didn't have work experience. We had to get a real job and work eight hours a day.
ALEX: ______
______

Write your own answer.

12 Two cartoons

Find the right caption for the cartoons.

1. "You'll have to look harder than that to find a job, son."
2. "I don't think much of your work experience, Eric."
3. What's for lunch today, Eric?

13 Preparing for an interview – what to do

Simon is nervous about an interview for a job next week. His father gives him some advice.

A *Complete the sentences using the phrases in the box.*

Remember to ... Don't forget to ... You mustn't ... You should never ... Make sure you (don't) ...	~~wear smart, clean clothes.~~ wear your trainers or sneakers. go to the hairdresser's. go to bed early the night before. find out where the company is. get information about the company. think of answers to questions they might ask. look at the person you are talking to. thank the person for the interview.

1. Remember to wear smart, clean clothes.
2. You mustn't
3. ____________________
4. ____________________
5. ____________________
6. ____________________
7. ____________________
8. ____________________
9. ____________________

B *What do you think of his father's advice?* ____________________

C *What should Simon do with his mobile phone? Write a tip for him.* ____________________

D Simon's careers advisor also gave him some tips on what to do at the interview.
Rewrite the sentences. Use the words in the box.

Try to ... • Try not to ... • It's a good idea to ... • It isn't a good idea to ...

1. Don't be late for the interview. Try not to be late for the interview. Try to be there on time.
2. Don't answer questions with 'Yes' or 'No'. ____________________
3. Don't talk about your weaknesses. ____________________
4. Don't say things about yourself that are not true. ____________________

14 Diana's interview

Sports Oasis is a popular leisure centre. It wants to employ a young person as an instructor. The manager, Colin Evans, invited Diana for an interview. The interview didn't go well. What mistakes did Diana make?
Read the interview carefully. Mark Diana's mistakes in the text. Write your answers in full sentences.

MR EVANS: Good morning, Diana. My name is Colin Evans. Welcome to Sports Oasis. The interview was planned for ten o'clock.
It's almost eleven.
DIANA: I'm sorry I'm late, Mr Colins. I missed the bus.
MR EVANS: My name is Colin Evans …
What do you know about Sports Oasis?
DIANA: Not much. It's a sports and leisure centre.
MR EVANS: I read in your CV that you are a member of the CPC judo club.
Tell me something about that.
DIANA: I stopped going there when I was twelve.
But I'm still a member.
MR EVANS: Oh, I see. Well, do you do any other sports?
DIANA: Yes.
MR EVANS: Have you had any work experience?
Have you ever taught things to adults?
DIANA: Well, I often taught people to swim when I was a part-time lifeguard at the local swimming pool.
MR EVANS: So, why do you think you would be a good instructor?
DIANA: Because I learn things quickly. You see, I want to work as an instructor abroad, soon.
MR EVANS: Have you had a job before?
DIANA: Yes, I had a job for a month. But I didn't like my boss.
MR EVANS: Do you have any questions about the job?
DIANA: Yes. How many days holiday do I get?
MR EVANS: Well, we'll discuss that if …
DIANA: Sorry. My mobile phone is ringing.
Can I quickly send a text message?

1. *Diana was late for the interview.*
2. *She got the name of the manager wrong.*
3. ______
4. ______
5. ______
6. ______
7. ______
8. ______
9. ______

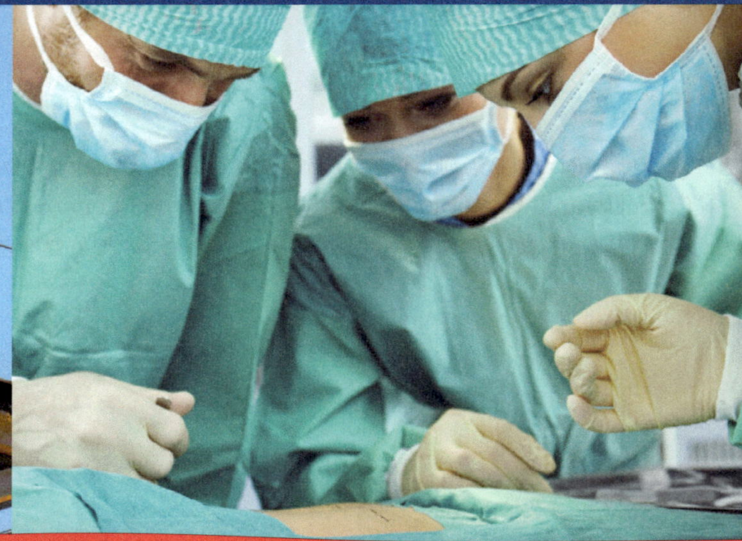

People at work

About 30 million people work in the UK economy. Some jobs are more popular than others.

1 Different types of work

Look at the statistics. How many people work in these industries? What jobs do they do?

2,200,000*	Construction industry
2,000,000*	Travel and tourism
1,300,000*	The National Health Service
1,250,000*	Finance
620,000*	Leisure, sport and recreation
250,000*	Hairdressing and beauty

* number of workers

beauty therapist • carer • carpenter • bank clerk • coach • electrician • fitness instructor • receptionist • nurse • tour guide • roofer • doctor • accountant • lifeguard • steward/stewardess • plumber • hairdresser • travel agent

1. 2.2 million people ______ work in the construction industry.
   They do jobs such as ______________________________.
2. ______________________________ in travel and tourism.
   They do jobs such as ______________________________.
3. ______________________________ in the National Health Service.
   They do jobs such as ______________________________.
4. ______________________________
   ____
5. ______________________________
   ____
6. ______________________________
   ____

2 Kate Johnson – a trainee hairdresser in Wales

In Britain about 250,000 people work in the hairdressing and beauty industry. In this industry it is important to make people look good and feel good. You need to be creative, hard-working and you must be able to listen to customers! Kate is training to be a hairdresser in a popular salon in Wales.

"Hi, I'm Kate. No, I'm not a punk! I'm a hair stylist at 'Short Cuts' – that's the trendiest salon in Cardiff. We specialise in young styles. My boss doesn't mind if my hair style is a bit wild. He says customers can see that I am creative!
I'm still a trainee. I work long hours to learn about cutting and colouring hair. I've already learned to do some fantastic styles. My boss says that if I work hard, he'll take me to the London Hair Show next year.
There's no time to be bored in this job. I'm always busy. On my days in the salon I have to wash and dry customers' hair. I also have to clean up, make tea for customers, work at reception. I like answering the phone and making appointments. I meet lots of different customers who often tell me stories about their lives and their problems. It's just as exciting as a soap opera on TV!
I work five days a week from 10 am to 6 pm. Mondays are usually free. The downside of the job is that I have to stand all day. My legs really ache at the end of the day. One day I would like to have my own salon and be my own boss."

A *Find the information from the text that tells you about:*

1. the opinion of Kate's boss: ______
2. the different jobs she has to do: ______
______
3. her working hours: ______
4 Mondays: ______
5. the downside and problems: ______
6. her dream: ______

B *Ask Kate three questions. Use three different question words (where, when, what, etc).*

1. ______
2. ______
3. ______

C *Look at these words and write sentences about Kate's job.*

1. Kate / long hours / learn / cut / colour hair
______
2. She / no time / bored / salon / always busy
______
3. She / meet / different people / stories / their lives / problems
______

3 Mike Sears – a lock keeper on the river Trent

If you want to spend all or part of your working day outdoors, there is a huge choice of careers. Mike Sears saw an advert for a job as a lock keeper. He had no experience, but he applied for the job and got it.

"I work for British Waterways. They trained me to do this job.
I work on the River Trent and my job is to help boats to pass through the lock from one part of the river to the next. The lock is on a tidal river so boats can only sail through the lock when the river is at a certain level. Boat owners have to phone me 24 hours before they use the lock and I tell them when the gates will be open. I read the tide table so I know when the tide is coming in or going out.
I also look after the lock and I oil all the equipment and make sure everything is working well. I take rubbish out of the river and clean the area round the lock. I enjoy the job because I work outside in a beautiful environment. The downside is that it's a lonely job. I work alone most days, but I talk to the people on the boats when they come through the lock. My hours are not regular because I have to work with the tides. In summer I can work from 6 am to 9 pm. I also work weekends but I get days off during the week."

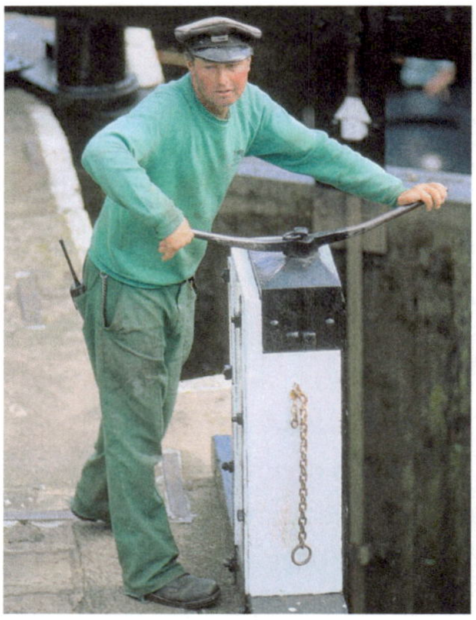

A Here is a pipe made of nine words from the text. *Find the words and write them.*

locktideriverboatphoneequipmentenvironmentsummerweekends

____

B Mike talked to his friend, David. Here are the answers to his questions. *Write David's questions.*

DAVID: *How did you find this job?*

MIKE: I saw a job advert for a lock keeper on the Internet. So I applied, and I got it.

DAVID: ____

MIKE: No, I didn't. It wasn't necessary as British Waterways trained me.

DAVID: ____

MIKE: No, I can only open the gates at certain times during the day. I have to check the tide tables.

DAVID: ____

MIKE: I look after the lock. I oil the equipment. I also take rubbish out of the river.

DAVID: ____

MIKE: I often talk to the people on the boats when they come through the lock.

DAVID: ____

MIKE: Yes, I do. But if that happens, I get some days off during the week.

C *Describe a lock keeper in your own words.*

____

____

4 Kevin Adams – a nursery assistant

Are you energetic, caring and patient? There are many jobs where you can work with young children. Kevin works as a nursery assistant. Here's what he thinks about his job.

"I haven't stopped all day! When you're looking after lots of four-year-olds, every day is a busy day. One little boy, Liam, was sick today, and I had to clean up. Yuk!
I work from 7.50 am to 4.30 pm. Before the children arrive, I check that all the toys and equipment are in good condition. In our nursery we always have a weekly theme and we organise most of our activities around it. This week we have chosen 'home life'.
After the children have gone home, I feel exhausted. But I have to stay here and tidy up. As a nursery assistant you must be patient, but you must also make clear rules. I have always wanted to work with children – and you really must like being with children to do this job. It's often hectic and loud, but there are more good things than bad things about the job. Children are curious. When they have learned to do something new, they are so happy and proud. You should see their faces!"

A *Read the introduction and the text and find the adjectives to describe …*

1. a typical day in the nursery ____________ ____________ ____________
2. a nursery assistant ____________ ____________ ____________
3. how an assistant feels at the end of a day ____________
4. children ____________
5. how children feel when they learn to do something ____________ ____________

B What did Kevin say to one of the parents at the end of the day? *Use the present perfect.*

1. It *has been* ____________ (be) very busy today. We ____________ (not stop) all day.
2. Liam ____________ (be) sick, but we ____________ (clean) his clothes. He's fine now.
3. We ____________ (check) all the toys. There is no dangerous equipment.
4. This week we ____________ (choose) 'home life' as our theme.
5. When the children ____________ (go home), we are all really exhausted.

C This is what Kevin must do today. He has already done some of the things, but he hasn't done everything yet. *Make sentences. Use the present perfect.*

1. *He hasn't made an Easter card with group one yet.*
2. ____________
3. ____________
4. ____________
5. ____________

– make an Easter card with group one
– practise the new song ✓
– write a letter to the parents
– fill the paint bottles
– phone Liam's mother ✓

5 Olivia Williams – a window dresser

Olivia is 21. She did a college course for two years in Display and now she works as a window dresser at a London store. *Read what she says about her job.*

Was it the job you wanted?
"It wasn't my dream, no, but I love my job. At school I was good at art. I was good at making 3D models of rooms and buildings. So I went to college and got a qualification in Display."

What are your working hours?
"We usually work five days a week, from 9 am until 6 pm. It's important to be punctual, and we have to be flexible, too. At Christmas and other busy times of the year we have to come in on Saturdays. You have to be a hard worker in this job."

What's your working week like?
"Mondays are boring. We have to tidy up the shop displays after a busy Saturday. The other days are cool. We work on the window displays and shop displays. I work in a team most of the time, but I often have to do a display on my own. I love that."

What's the best bit of your job?
"The displays. I really love doing small displays on my own. I like using my own ideas and being creative with colours and objects."

And the worst bit?
"Sometimes customers walk into the window displays and mess them up. It's really annoying and we have to be polite to them! The pay isn't very good, so it helps if you really love your work."

What about your future?
"I would like to be the display manager here. That's my dream now."

A *Find information in the text which tells you …*

1. what Olivia did well at school.

____

2. about Olivia's working hours.

____

3. why she has to be flexible in her job.

____

4. why Mondays are boring.

____

5. why Olivia likes working on small displays.

____

6. about her salary.

____

7. what Olivia's dream is.

____

Mr Denton, Olivia's boss, is talking to a colleague about Olivia.

B *Read what Mr Denton says and tick ☑ the best words to describe Olivia.*

1. "Olivia is never angry with annoying customers. She is friendly to everyone."

   Olivia is busy. ☐ Olivia is polite. ☐ Olivia is cool. ☐

2. "When there is lots of work to do, Olivia often comes earlier or leaves later."

   She is fast. ☐ She is flexible. ☐ She is creative. ☐

3. "She always starts work at the right time. She is never late."

   She is punctual. ☐ She is ready. ☐ She is friendly. ☐

4. "She has no problem with busy days and long hours."

   She is a lazy worker. ☐ She is a team worker. ☐ She is a hard worker. ☐

5. "I think she has a great future in her job."

   He can see her as a dreamer. ☐ He can see her as a display manager. ☐

   He can see her as a window cleaner. ☐

C Is Mr Denton pleased, or not pleased with Olivia's work? *What do you think?*

____

D *Complete the sentences about Olivia and her job. Find the missing words.*

on her own • ~~at school~~ • good at making • in a team • use her own ideas • went to college • walk into the window displays • be creative with colours and objects

1. When she was *at school* Olivia really enjoyed art.
2. She was very ______________________ 3D models of rooms and buildings.
3. When she left school, she ______________________ and got a qualification in Display.
4. Most of the time she works ______________ but sometimes she does a display ______________.
5. She loves doing small displays because she can ______________________ and ______________

   ____.
6. It's really annoying when customers ______________________ and mess them up.

E *Find the odd word out.*

1. punctual, <u>inside</u>, polite, creative
2. window, door, building, roof
3. New Year, Saturday, Easter, Christmas
4. qualification, school, college, university
5. art, geography, maths, colour
6. week, calendar, year, month

"You think this is FUNNY?! I'm 38! I live with my mother! I got a college degree!"

6 Starting your own business

When they were young men, Ben Cohen and Jerry Greenfield didn't know what they wanted to do. So they started to make ice cream. It became a big ice cream business.

A *Complete this story about Ben, Jerry and their ice cream business. Use the correct form of the verbs.*

borrow • buy • call • eat • give • have no idea • become • sell • open • organise • ~~make and sell~~

1. In 1978 they made and sold ice cream in their first shop in a town called Burlington.
2. They ________ $4000 from the bank to pay for the shop and equipment.
3. They ________ what name to use for their product, so they ________ it Ben and Jerry's Homemade Ice Cream.
4. After their first year they ________ a Free Ice Cream Day and ________ free ice cream to all their customers.
5. As their business grew, they ________ their ice cream to shops and restaurants in the area.
6. Ben and Jerry ________ so much of their own ice cream that they ________ very fat.
7. After 10 years Ben and Jerry ________ 88 shops in 18 states.
8. Today, Ben and Jerry's ice cream is ________ all over the world.

B Would you like to start your own business? Why? What would you like to do? *Write three to five sentences.*

____

____

____

7 Say it in English

How would you say or ask these things in English? *Write your answers.*

1. Frage, welchen Beruf jemand hat. What's your job?
2. Frage, was jemandem am meisten an seiner Arbeit gefällt. ________
3. Sage, dass deine Freundin Ina arbeitslos ist. ________
4. Sage, dass du einen neuen Job suchst. ________
5. Frage, welche Qualifikationen man für den Job braucht. ________

8 Tools and equipment for the job

A *Look at the tools and equipment. Find the meaning of the words in the box. Match the words with the illustrations.*

camera	_____	frying pan	_____	ladder	_____	scissors	_____
chainsaw	_____	hammer	_____	laptop	_____	screwdriver	_____
comb	_____	hosepipe	_____	oil	_____	spade	_____
desk	_____	knife	_____	phone	_____	spanners	_____

B *Write down the tools or the equipment you need for each job (two things).*

1. a photographer ____________________
2. a carpenter ____________________
3. a gardener ____________________
4. a cook ____________________
5. a receptionist ____________________
6. a mechanic ____________________
7. a fireman ____________________
8. a hairdresser ____________________

9 What are they used for?

cut down trees • cook food • ~~dry hair~~ • hit nails into wood • repair engines • dig in the garden • take photos • cut hair

1. A towel is used for drying hair.
2. Scissors are ____________________
3. A camera ____________________
4. A frying pan ____________________
5. A spanner ____________________
6. A chainsaw ____________________
7. A hammer ____________________
8. A spade ____________________

10 Safety at work

Safety at work is very important. The people in the photos have dangerous jobs and they are all wearing clothes which protect them or they are using equipment which protects them.

A *Find the following words in the vocabulary list at the end of the book. Look at the photos and say who is wearing each thing.*

boots	________	an ear muff	________
a face shield	________	a hard hat	________
gloves	________	overalls	________
goggles	________		

B Why do people wear the things in the photos? What do they want to protect? *Make sentences with these words.*

1. head: You wear a hard hat to protect your head.
2. ears: ________
3. hands: ________
4. eyes: ________
5. face: ________
6. feet: ________
7. normal clothes: ________

11 Signs

Signs in your workplace give you important information and tell you about dangers.

A What do the signs mean? *Choose an answer from the box and write it next to sign.*

> You must wear goggles, an ear muff and boots. • You can buy hats here. • No mobiles! • You mustn't go in here. • You must wear a hard hat. • You mustn't make long phone calls here. • You mustn't go out here. • Don't go to the toilet! • You can stop a machine with this button. • Everyone must meet here if there is a fire. • You can use this to put out a small fire. • You can't work here if you wear glasses. •

1. 

2. 

3. 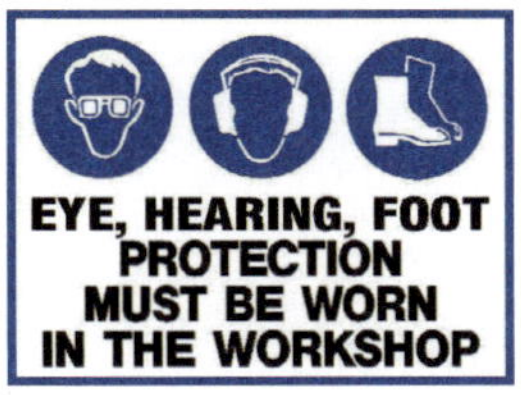

4. 

5. 

6. 

B *Use your own words to tell somebody the meaning of these signs.*

1. 

2. 

Wortschatz

Englische Laute

Mitlaute

[b]	bed	[p]	picture
[d]	day	[r]	red
[ð]	the	[s]	six
[f]	family	[ʃ]	she
[g]	go	[t]	ten
[ŋ]	morning	[tʃ]	lunch
[h]	house	[v]	video
[j]	you	[w]	we, one
[k]	can, milk	[z]	easy
[l]	letter	[ʒ]	revision
[m]	man	[dʒ]	page
[n]	no	[θ]	thank you

Selbstlaute

[ɑ:]	car
[æ]	apple
[e]	pen
[ə]	again
[ɜ:]	girl
[ʌ]	but
[ɪ]	it
[i]	happy
[i:]	teacher
[ɒ]	dog
[ɔ:]	ball
[ʊ]	book
[u]	January
[u:]	too, two

Doppellaute

[aɪ]	I, my
[aʊ]	now, mouse
[eɪ]	name, they
[eə]	there, pair
[ɪə]	here, idea
[əʊ]	hello
[ɔɪ]	boy
[ʊə]	sure

[:] der vorangehende Laut ist lang, z. B. *you* [ju:]

['] die folgende Silbe wird betont, z. B. *hello* [hə'ləʊ]

Communication

2	**text message**	['tekst mesɪdʒ]	SMS (-Nachricht)
3	**radio waves**	['reɪdiəʊ weɪvz]	Radiowellen
	communication satellite	[kəmju:nɪ'keɪʃən sætəlaɪt]	Fernmeldesatellit
	invent	[ɪn'vent]	erfinden
	connect people	[kə'nekt pi:pl]	Menschen (miteinander) verbinden
	popular	['pɒpjələ]	beliebt
4	**computer skills**	[kəm'pju:tə skɪlz]	Computerkentnisse
	build	[bɪld]	*hier:* zusammen bauen
	repair	[rɪ'peə]	reparieren
	spreadsheet software	['spredʃi:t sɒftweə]	Tabellenkalkulationsprogramm
	type	[taɪp]	tippen (auf einer Tastatur)
	accurate	['ækjərət]	genau, akkurat
	design programme	['dɪzaɪn prəʊgræm]	Bildbearbeitungsprogramm
	network computers	['netwɜ:k kəm'pju:təz]	ein Computernetzwerk aufbauen
5	**hard disk/hard drive**	[hɑ:d dɪsk; hɑ:d draɪv]	Festplatte
	keyboard	['ki:bɔ:d]	Tastatur
	monitor	['mɒnɪtə]	Bildschirm/der Monitor
	scanner	['skænə]	Scanner
	mouse	[maʊs]	Maus
	(laser)printer	['leɪzə prɪntə]	(Laser-)Drucker
	headset	['hedset]	Headset/Kopfhörer
	loudspeaker	[laʊdspi:kə]	Lautsprecher
	webcam	['webkæm]	Webcam

	wireless Internet	['waɪələs ɪntənet]	drahtloser Internetzugang
7	**in my opinion**	[ɪn maɪ ə'pɪnjən]	meiner Meinung nach
	as soon as possible	[əz su:n əz pɒsəbl]	so bald wie möglich
8	**apply for a job**	['əplaɪ fr ə dʒɒb]	sich für/um eine Stelle bewerben
	Would you be kind enough to ...	[wəd ju bi kaɪnd ɪ'nʌf tə]	Wären Sie so freundlich und ...
	I look forward to hearing from you.	[aɪ lʊk fɔ:wəd tə hɪəriŋ frɒm ju:]	Ich freue mich darauf von Ihnen zu hören.
	Please find enclosed ...	[pli:z faɪnd ɪn'kləʊzd]	Anbei erhalten Sie .../Beiliegend finden Sie ...
	Please accept my apologies about ...	[pli:z ək'sept maɪ ə'pɒlədʒiz ə'baʊt]	Bitte entschuldigen Sie den/die/das ...
9	**customer**	['kʌstəmər]	Kunde/Kundin
	health product	['helθ prɒdəkt]	Gesundheitsartikel
	manager	['mænɪdʒə]	Abteilungsleiter/Betriebsleiter/Geschäftsführer
	reply	[rɪ'plaɪ]	Antwort
	deliver	[dɪ'lɪvə]	liefern/ausliefern
	delivery costs	[dɪ'lɪvəri kɒsts]	Lieferkosten
	postage	['pəʊstɪdʒ]	Porto
	receive	[rɪ'sɪ:v]	empfangen/bekommen/erhalten
	to be annoyed about something	[tə bɪ ə'nɔɪd ə'baʊt 'sʌmθɪŋ]	wegen einer Sache verärgert sein
10	**Thank you for calling.**	[θæŋkju fə 'kɔ:lɪŋ]	Vielen Dank für Ihren Anruf.
	Just a moment.	[dʒʌst ə 'məʊmənt]	Einen Augenblick, bitte.
	Who's calling, please?	[hu:z kɔ:lɪŋ pli:z]	Wer ist bitte am Apparat?
	Can I take a message?	[kən aɪ teɪk ə mesɪdʒ]	Kann ich jemandem etwas ausrichten?
	I'll be happy to give him your message.	[aɪl bi 'hæpi tə gɪv ɪm jʊəmesɪdʒ]	Ich richte es ihm gern aus.
	Caroline Best speaking.	['kærəlaɪn best spi:kɪŋ]	Caroline Best am Apparat.
11	**caller**	['kɔ:lə]	Anrufer/Anruferin
	mobile (phone) *(BE)*	[məʊbaɪl 'fəʊn]	Mobiltelefon; Handy
	cell phone *(AE)*	[sel 'fəʊn]	
	Pay As You Go (mobile)	[peɪ əz ju: gəʊ]	Prepaid Handy
	ring tone	['rɪŋ təʊn]	Klingelton
	username	['ju:zəneɪm]	Benutzerkennwort

Career plans

12	**computer engineer**	[kəm'pju:tə endʒɪ'nɪə]	Computertechniker/Computertechnikerin
	cook	[kʊk]	Koch/Köchin
	beauty therapist	['bju:ti θerəpist]	Kosmetikerin
	plumber	['plʌmə]	Klempner/Klempnerin
	police officer	[pə'li:s ɒfɪsə]	Polizist/Polizistin
	sales assistant	[seɪlz ə'sɪstənt]	Ladenverkäufer/- verkäuferin
	(car) mechanic	[kɑ: mɪ'kænɪk]	(Auto-) Mechaniker/Mechanikerin
	pilot	['paɪlət]	Pilot/Pilotin
	electrician	[elɪk'trɪʃən]	Elektriker/Elektrikerin
	truck driver	[trʌk draɪvə]	Lasterfahrer/-fahrerin
	hairdresser	['heədresə]	Friseur/Friseurin
	soldier	['səʊldʒə]	Soldat/Soldatin
	secretary	['sekrətəri]	Sekretär/Sekretärin

	builder	[ˈbɪldə]	Baufachmann; Baumeister/-in
	photographer	[fəˈtɒgrəfə]	Fotograf/Fotografin
	painter and decorator	[ˈpeɪntə ənd ˈdekəreɪtə]	Maler/-in und Lackierer/-in
	lifeguard	[ˈlaɪfgɑ:d]	Bademeister/Bademeisterin
	nurse/male nurse	[nɜ:s; meɪl nɜ:s]	Krankenpfleger/Krankenschwester
	(hotel) receptionist	[həʊtel rɪˈsepʃənɪst]	Empfangsmitarbeiter/-mitarbeiterin
	carer	[keərə]	Pfleger/Pflegerin
	work long hours	[wɜ:k lɒŋ aʊəz]	Überstunden machen; sehr lange arbeiten
	break down	[breɪk daʊn]	*hier:* eine (Auto)Panne haben
	arrest a criminal	[əˈrest ə ˈkrɪmɪnəl]	einen Verbrecher festnehmen
13	**actor/actress**	[ˈæktə; ˈæktrəs]	Schauspieler/Schauspielerin
	caretaker	[ˈkeəteɪkə]	Hausmeister/Hausmeisterin
	dancer	[ˈdɑ:nsə]	Tänzer/Tänzerin
	doctor	[ˈdɒktə]	Arzt/Ärztin
	farmer	[ˈfɑ:mə]	Bauer/Bäuerin
	goalkeeper	[ˈgəʊlki:pə]	Torwart/Torwartin
	headteacher	[hedˈti:tʃə]	Schulleiter/-in; Rektor/-in
	vet's assistant	[vets əˈsɪstənt]	Tierarzthelfer/-in
	waiter/waitress	[ˈweɪtə; ˈweɪtrəs]	Kellner/-in
	lorry (*plural:* lorries)	[ˈlɒri]	Lastwagen
	daily routine	[ˈdeɪli ru:ˈti:n]	Tagesablauf
14	**creative**	[kriˈeɪtɪv]	kreativ
	practical	[ˈpræktɪkəl]	praktisch veranlagt
	organised	[ˈɔ:gənaɪzd]	gut organisiert
	outgoing	[aʊtˈgəʊɪŋ]	kontaktfreudig
	caring	[keərɪŋ]	sozial; mitfühlend
	committed	[kəˈmɪtɪd]	engagiert
	(be a) born leader	[bɪ: ə bɔ:n ˈli:də]	eine Führernatur (sein)
	team player	[ˈti:m pleɪə]	jemand, der gut im Team arbeitet
	under pressure	[ʌndə ˈpreʃə]	unter Druck
	be your own boss = have your own business	[bɪ jər əʊn bɒs]	selbstständig sein
	construction company	[kənˈstrʌkʃən kʌmpəni]	Baufirma; Baugesellschaft
	ring tone recorder	[ˈrɪŋtəʊn rɪˈkɔ:də]	Tontechniker, der Klingeltöne für Handys aufnimmt.
	chewing gum buster	[ˈtʃu:ɪŋgʌm bʌstə]	Kaugummi-Bekämpfer/-Entferner
	profession	[prəˈfeʃən]	Beruf
	annoying	[əˈnɔɪŋ]	ärgerlich
	successful	[səkˈsesfəl]	erfolgreich
	success	[səkˈses]	der Erfolg
15	**leisure centre**	[ˈleʒər sentə]	Sport- und Freizeitzentrum
	earn	[ɜ:n]	verdienen
	train somebody (to become a ...)	[treɪn sʌmbədi]	(jemanden als ...) ausbilden
	unemployed	[ʌnɪmˈplɔɪd]	arbeitslos; erwerbslos
	reporter	[rɪˈpɔ:tə]	Reporter/-in; Berichterstatter/-in
16	**train (to be a hairdresser)**	[treɪn tə bɪ: ə ˈheədresə]	eine Ausbildung (zum Friseur) machen

	work part-time	[wɜ:k pɑ:t'taɪm]	teilzeit arbeiten
	my perfect job	[maɪ 'pɜ:fɪkt dʒɒb]	die perfekte Stelle für mich
	start your own company	[stɒt yʊə əʊn kʌmpəni]	eine eigene Firma gründen
	custom-build something	[kʌstəmbɪld 'sʌmθɪŋ]	etwas einzeln anfertigen
	gardener	[gɑ:dənə]	Gärtner/-in
	(be) outside	[bɪ: aʊt'saɪd]	draußen (sein); im Freien (sein)
	well-paid	[wel peɪd]	gut bezahlt
	(*opposite:* badly -paid; low-paid)	['bædli peɪd; ləʊ peɪd]	(schlecht bezahlt)
17	**career**	[kə'rɪə]	Beruf; Berufsleben; beruflicher Werdegang; Karriere
	advantage	[əd'vɑ:ntɪdʒ]	Vorteil
	disadvantage	[dɪsəd'vɑ:ntɪdʒ]	Nachteil
	ask somebody for advice	[əd'vaɪs]	jemanden um Rat bitten
	give somebody advice		jemandem Ratschläge erteilen
	personality	[pɜ:sən'æləti]	Persönlichkeit
	work experience	[wɜ:k ɪk'spɪəriənts]	*hier:* Arbeitserfahrung; Berufserfahrung; Praxiserfahrung
	skill	[skɪl]	Fähigkeit; Fertigkeit; Qualifikation
	ability (*plural:* abilities)	[ə'bɪləti]	Fähigkeit
	(be) available	[ə'veɪləbl]	zur Auswahl stehen
	working life	[wɜ:kɪŋ laɪf]	Arbeitsleben; Berufsleben
	job market	[dʒɒb 'mɑ:kɪt]	Arbeitsmarkt
	Do you call this a three-course meal?	[θri: kɔ:s mi:l]	Das hier soll ein Drei-Gänge Menü sein?
	complain (about something)	[kəm'pleɪn]	sich (über etwas) beschweren
18	**careers advisor**	[kə'rɪəz əd'vaɪzə]	Berufsberater/-in
	apprenticeship	[ə'prentɪʃɪp]	Ausbildung; Lehre
	sound engineer	[saʊnd endʒɪ'nɪə]	Tontechniker/-in
	colleague	['kɒli:g]	(Arbeits)Kollege/Kollegin
	salary	[sæləri]	Gehalt
	employee	[ɪm'plɔɪi:]	Arbeitnehmer/-in; Angestellter/Angestellte
	wage	[weɪdʒ]	(Arbeits)Lohn
	employer	[ɪm'plɔɪə]	Arbeitgeber/-in
	minimum wage	[mɪnɪməm weɪdʒ]	Mindestlohn
	tax	[tæks]	Steuer
19	**advert = job advert**	['ædvɜ:t]	Stellenanzeige
	be willing to do something	[bɪ: 'wɪlɪŋ]	bereit sein, etwas zu tun
	work outdoors	[wɜ:k aʊt'dɔ:z]	im Freien arbeiten
	tool	[tu:l]	Werkzeug
	physical work	['fɪzɪkəl wɜ:k]	körperliche Arbeit
	flexible hours	['fleksɪbl aʊəz]	flexible Arbeitszeit
	steward	['stju:əd]	Steward; Schiffskellner
	candidate	['kændɪdət]	*hier:* Bewerber/-in
	bonus	[bəʊnəs]	Bonus; Gehaltszuschlag
	full-time	[fʊl'taɪm]	(in) Vollzeit
	full-time job		Vollzeitstelle
	work full-time		Vollzeit arbeiten
	... is a must.	[ɪz ə mʌst]	... ist ein Muss (*hier:* wird erwartet)

	(be) hard-working	[hɑ:d'wɜ:kɪŋ]	fleißig (sein)
	shift	[ʃɪft]	Schicht; Dienst
	work shifts; do shift work		Schicht arbeiten
	Salary meets minimum wage.	[sæləri mi:ts mɪnɪməm weɪdʒ]	Mindestlohn garantiert.
	tip	[tɪp]	Trinkgeld
	quality	['kwɒləti]	*hier:* Eigenschaft
20	**start a college course**	[kɒlɪdʒ kɔ:s]	eine Ausbildung an einer Berufs(fach)schule beginnen
	work abroad	[ə'brɔ:d]	im Ausland (arbeiten)
	go abroad		ins Ausland (gehen)
	volunteer	[vɒlən'tɪər]	Freiwillige
	three-month project	['prɒdʒekt]	ein dreimonatiges Projekt
	accomodation	[əkɒmə'deɪʃən]	Unterkunft
	au pair	[əʊ'peə]	Au-Pair Mädchen/Junge
	look after	[lʊk 'ɑ:ftə]	sich um jemanden kümmern; auf jemanden aufpassen
	conditions	[kən'dɪʃənz]	Bedingungen

Applications and interviews

22	**dos and don'ts**	[du:z ən dəʊnts]	Dinge, die man tun und nicht tun sollte.
	letter of application	[letə əv æplɪ'keɪʃən]	Bewerbungsschreiben/-brief
	trainee	[treɪ'ni:]	jemand, der eine Ausbildung macht
	trainee cook	[treɪni: 'kʊk]	jemand, der eine Ausbildung zum Koch macht
	CV (Curriculum Vitae)	[si:'vi:]	Lebenslauf
	make a good impression	[gʊd ɪm'preʃən]	einen guten Eindruck machen
	invite somebody for an interview	[ɪn'vaɪt 'sʌmbədi fər ən 'ɪntəvju:]	jemanden zum Vorstellungsgespräch einladen
23	**update your CV**	['ʌpdeɪt jə si:'vi:]	deinen Lebenslauf auf den neusten Stand bringen
	address with postcode	['ədres wɪð 'pəʊstkəʊd]	Adresse mit Postleitzahl
	brief summary	[bri:f 'sʌməri]	kurze Zusammenfassung
	attend school	[ə'tend sku:l]	eine Schule besuchen
	qualifications	[kwɒlɪfɪ'keɪʃənz]	*hier:* Zeugnisse; Qualifikationen
	work experience	[wɜ:k ɪk'spɪəriənts]	*hier:* Berufspraktikum
	additional	[ə'dɪʃənəl]	weitere; zusätzliche
	sporting achievements	['spɔ:tɪŋ ə'tʃi:vmənt]	sportliche Leistungen
	language skills	['læŋgwɪdʒ skɪlz]	Fremdsprachenkenntnisse
	motivated	['məʊtɪveɪtɪd]	motiviert
	reliable	[rɪ'laɪəbl]	zuverlässig
	good sense of humour	[gʊd sents əv 'hju :mə]	ein guter Sinn für Humor
	be keen on	[bɪ ki:n ɒn]	etwas sehr gerne tun
	member	['membə]	Mitglied
	(department) store	[dɪ'pɑ:tmənt stɔ:]	Kaufhaus; sehr großer Laden
	mother tongue	[mʌðər tʌŋ]	Muttersprache
	equivalent	[ɪ'kwɪvələnt]	Entsprechung
25	**sales personnel**	[seɪlz pɜ:sən'el]	Verkaufspersonal
	main branch	[meɪn brɑ:ntʃ]	Hauptgeschäftsstelle

	qualifications	[kwɒlɪfɪ'keɪʃənz]	*hier:* Eignung; Qualifizierung
	basic skills	[beɪsɪk skɪlz]	Grundkenntnisse
	cover letter (*also:* covering letter)	['kʌvə letə] ['kʌvərɪŋ letə]	Begleitbrief; Bewerbungsschreiben; Anschreiben
	headquarters	[hed'kwɔ:təz]	Zentrale
	expand	[ɪk'spænd]	*hier:* Geschäft erweitern
	a wide range of	[ə waɪd reɪndʒ əv]	eine große Auswahl an
	consumer electronic products	[kən'sju:mə elek'trɒnɪk 'prɒdʌkts]	Unterhaltungselektronik
	electrical household appliance	[ɪ'lektrɪkəl 'haʊshəʊld ə'plaɪənts]	Elektro-Haushaltsgerät
26	**vacancy (*plural:* vacancies)**	['veɪkəntsi]	Stellenangebot; offene Stelle
	polite	[pə'laɪt]	höflich
27	**Human Resources Department**	['hju:mən rɪ'zɔ:sɪz dɪ'pɑ:tmənt]	Personalabteilung
	(be a) hard worker	[hɑ:d 'wɜ:kə]	fleißig sein
	opportunity	[ɒpə'tju:nəti]	Gelegenheit
	(be) available for	[ə'veɪləbl]	für etwas zur Verfügung stehen
	passion	['pæʃən]	Leidenschaft
	advertising assistant	['ædvətaɪzɪŋ ə'sɪstənt]	Werbeassisten/-assistentin
	(be) prepared to do sth	[prɪ'peəd]	bereit (sein) etwas zu tun
28	**advertising department**	['ædvətaɪzɪŋ dɪ'pɑ:tmənt]	Werbeabteilung (in einer Firma)
	television company	['telɪvɪʒən 'kʌmpəni]	Fersehunternehmen
29	**employ somebody**	[ɪm'plɔɪ 'sʌmbədi]	jemanden anstellen; beschäftigen
	It's about time!	[ɪts ə'baʊt taɪm]	Das wurde aber auch Zeit!
	lazy	['leɪzi]	faul
	(be) impressed	[ɪm'prest]	beeindruckt sein
	I don't think much of ...	[aɪ dəʊnt θɪŋk mʌtʃ əv]	Ich halte nicht sehr viel von ...
30	**smart clothes**	[smɑ:t kləʊðz]	schicke Kleidung
	weakness	['wi:knəs]	Schwäche
31	**instructor**	[ɪn'strʌktə]	Lehrer/-in; Ausbilder/-in; Trainer/-in
	go well	[gəʊ wel]	gut laufen
	lifeguard	['laɪfgɑ:d]	Bademeister/-in
	local	['ləʊkəl]	örtlich

People at work

32	**construction industry**	[kən'strʌkʃən 'ɪndəstri]	Bauindustrie
	travel and tourism	['trævəl ən 'tʊərɪzəm]	Reise-und Touristikbranche
	National Health Service (NHS)	['næʃənəl helθ 'sɜ:vɪs]	staatlicher Gesundheitsdienst in Großbritannien
	finance	['faɪnænts]	Finanzwesen
	leisure, sport and recreation	['leʒər, spɔ:t ən rekri'eɪʃən]	Sport- und Freizeitindustrie
	carpenter	['kɑ:pəntə]	Tischler; Zimmermann/-frau
	bank clerk	['bæŋk klɑ:k]	Bankangestellter/Bankangestellte
	coach	[kəʊtʃ]	Trainer/-in
	fitness instructor	['fɪtnəs ɪn'strʌktə]	Fitnesstrainer/-in

	nurse	[nɜːs]	Krankenschwester
	tour guide	[tʊə gaɪd]	Reiseleiter/-in
	roofer	['ruːfə]	Dachdecker/-in
	accountant	[ə'kaʊntənt]	Buchhalter/-in
	travel agent	['trævəl eɪdʒənt]	Reisebürokaufmann/-frau
33	**hairdressing**	['heədresɪŋ]	Friseurberuf
	beauty	['bjuːti]	Schönheit
	industry	['ɪndəstri]	*hier:* Branche
	make somebody look good	[meɪk 'sʌmbədi lʊk gʊd]	jemanden verschönern
	salon	['sælɒn]	Friseursalon
	specialise in	['speʃəlaɪz ɪn]	spezializieren auf
	cutting and colouring	[kʌtɪŋ ən 'kʌlərɪŋ]	schneiden und färben/tönen
	(hair)style	['heəstaɪl]	Frisur
	appointment	[ə'pɔɪntmənt]	Termin
	downside of the job	['daʊnsaɪd]	die Nachteile der Arbeit/die weniger angenehme Seite der Arbeit
	ache	[eɪk]	wehtun; schmerzen
34	**lock keeper**	[lɒk 'kiːpə]	Schleusenwart
	tidal	['taɪdəl]	den Gezeiten unterworfen
	tide table	[taɪd 'teɪbl]	Gezeitenkalendar
	choice	[tʃɔɪs]	Auswahl
	unusual	[ʌn'juːʒəl]	ungewöhnlich; ausgefallen
	owner	[əʊnə]	Besitzer/-in
	own	[əʊn]	besitzen
	oil	[ɔɪl]	einölen; einfetten
	equipment	[ɪ'kwɪpmənt]	*hier:* die Geräte; die Anlage
	work (well)	[wɜːk wel]	*hier:* (gut) funktionieren
	environment	[ɪn'vaɪrənmənt]	*hier:* Umgebung
	regular	['regjələ]	regelmäßig
	(working) hours	[wɜːkɪŋ 'aʊəz]	Arbeitszeit
	have a day off	[hæv ə deɪ ɒf]	einen Tag frei haben
	take a day off	[teɪk ə deɪ ɒf]	einen Tag frei nehmen
35	**energetic**	[enə'dʒetɪk]	dynamisch; tatkräftig
	patient	['peɪʃənt]	geduldig
	nursery assistant *(BE)* **kindergarten assistant *(AE)***	['nɜːsəri ə'sɪstənt]	Kindergärtner/-in
	nursery (school)	['nɜːsəri skuːl]	Kindergarten
	I haven't stopped all day.	[aɪ 'hævənt stɒpt ɔːl deɪ]	Ich habe heute pausenlos gearbeitet.
	be sick *(BE)*	[biː sɪk]	sich übergeben
	be sick *(AE)*	[biː sɪk]	krank sein
	make rules	[meɪk ruːlz]	Regeln aufstellen
	theme	[θiːm]	Thema
	exhausted	[ɪg'zɔːstɪd]	erschöpft; völlig ermüdet
36	**window dresser**	['wɪndəʊ dresə]	Schaufensterdekorateur/-in; Schaufenstergestalter/-in
	Display	[dɪ'spleɪ]	Schaufensterdekoration; Schaufenstergestaltung
	punctual	['pʌŋktʃuəl]	pünktlich

	at busy times of the year	[ət 'bɪzi taɪmz əv ðə jɪə]	zu Hauptgeschäftszeiten
	shop display	[ʃɒp dɪ'spleɪ]	Dekoration im Verkaufsbereich eines Ladens
	window display	[wɪndəʊ dɪ'spleɪ]	Schaufensterdekoration
	on my own (on your own/ on his own/on our own/on their own)	[ən maɪ əʊn]	allein; ohne Hilfe; selbstständig
	mess up something	[mes ʌp sʌmθɪŋ]	etwas in Unordnung bringen; etwas durcheinander bringen
	It's annoying.	[ɪts ə'nɔɪɪŋ]	Es ist ärgerlich.
	display manager	[dɪ'spleɪ mænɪdʒə]	leitende(r) Dekorateur/-in
37	**annoying**	[ə'nɔɪɪŋ]	*hier:* lästig; nervig
	team worker	[ti:m 'wɜ:kə]	teamfähiger Arbeiter/teamfähige Arbeiterin
	see somebody as ...	[si: 'sʌmbədi əz]	sich jemanden vorstellen als ...
38	**start your own business**	[stɑ:t jər əʊn 'bɪznɪs]	ein Geschäft anfangen; ein Unternehmen gründen
	borrow (money)	[bɒrəʊ 'mʌni]	Geld aufnehmen
39	**chainsaw**	['tʃeɪnsɔ:]	Kettensäge
	comb	[kəʊm]	Kamm
	frying pan	[fraɪɪŋ pæn]	Bratpfanne
	hosepipe	['həʊzpaɪp]	Wasserschlauch
	knife	[naɪf]	*hier:* Kochmesser
	ladder	['lædə]	Leiter
	oil	[ɔɪl]	*hier:* Motoröl
	scissors	['sɪzəz]	Schere
	screwdriver	['skru:draɪvə]	Schraubendreher
	spade	[speɪd]	Spaten
	spanner	['spænə]	Schraubenschlüssel
	fireman/firewoman	['faɪəmən/'faɪəwʊmən]	Feuerwehrmann/-frau
	nail	[neɪl]	Nagel
	engine	['endʒɪn]	Motor
	take a photo	[teɪk ə 'fəʊtəʊ]	ein Foto machen
40	**safety**	['seɪfti]	Sicherheit
	protect	[prə'tekt]	schützen
	boots	[bu:ts]	Sicherheitsschuh
	face shield	[feɪs ʃi:ld]	Gesichtsschutzschild
	gloves	[glʌvz]	Handschuh
	goggles *(plural)*	['gɒglz]	Schutzbrille
	ear muff	[ɪər mʌf]	Ohrenschützer
	hard hat	[hɑ:d hæt]	Schutzhelm
	overalls *(plural)*	['əʊvərɔ:lz]	Arbeitsanzug; Arbeitskleidung; Latzhose
41	**sign**	[saɪn]	Schild
	workplace	['wɜ:kpleɪs]	Arbeitsplatz; Arbeitsstelle
	danger	['deɪndʒər]	Gefahr
	dangerous	['deɪndʒərəs]	gefährlich
	make a phone call	[meɪk ə fəʊn kɔ:l]	ein Telefongespräch führen; telefonieren
	put out (a fire)	[pʊt aʊt ə faɪə]	(ein Feuer) löschen

Lösungen

Communication

1 Communicating in different ways

Photo: laptop (for e-mail, MSN); newspaper; mobile phone; handheld computer (for example Blackberry; Palm)
Your ideas: letter by mail/post; carrier pigeon/homing pigeon (Brieftaube); television (including Video und DVD); radio; e-mail; MSN (instant message); computer Video telephone like Skype with a webcam;

2 What would you do?

Lösungsvorschlag:

2. If I wanted to chat online, I think I'd use a programme like ICQ/MSN Web Messenger, or I'd go onto schülerVZ or meinVZ (a site like Facebook).
3. If I wanted to find out more about a job, I'd use a search engine to check the Internet for information.
4. If I wanted to relax with my favourite music, I'd listen to my MP3-player/my I-Pod/music (that I have) on my computer.
5. If I wanted to tell my friends about my trips, I'd send an e-mail or I'd chat to them on schülerVZ/on meinVZ.

3 "Mr Watson, I want to see you!"

1. The first telephone was invented in the nineteenth century by an American, Alexander Graham Bell.
2. On March 10, 1876, he spoke through his new invention to his assistant,Thomas Watson, who was in the next room.
3. He said, „Mr Watson. Come here. I want to see you."
4. The earliest telephones had one wire, which could only connect two people.
5. Thirty years later telephone cables were laid under the sea from America to Britain.
6. In 1927 it was possible to call somebody in London from New York. The phones used radio waves.
7. In 1962 the first communications satellite was sent into space and people could talk all over the world.
8. As more and more people wanted phones, they were given their individual phone numbers.
9. During the 1970s and and 1980s car phones became very popular, but they were expensive.
10. However, in the 1990s mobile phones became much cheaper and millions of people could buy them. There are now about 4 billion mobile phones in the world.

4 What do you say in English?

2. I can make videos on my mobile (phone).
3. I'll ring you this afternoon.
4. I'll send you a text (message).
5. What did your new mobile (phone) cost?/How much was your new mobile (phone)?
6. Do you have/Have you got a new mobile number?
7. What do you pay per month?

5 Modern technology

Lösungsvorschlag:
I have learned how to use office software, but I've never used a design programme.
I've learned how to use spreadsheet software like Excel, but I can't use design programmes.
I have learned how to burn CDs and DVDs.
I've learned how to install software, but I don't know how to burn CDs and DVDs.
I'm good at building/repairing computers.
I'm really good at creating websites, but I can't type quickly and accurately. (My brother has to check it!)
I don't know how to repair computers.
I know/I don't know how to network computers.

6 Fourth word

1. speak 2. website 3. busy 4. switch on 5. cell phone 6. library 7. advertisement 8. headline 9. monitor

7 The multimedia computer

1. hard disk 2. keyboard 3. monitor 4. scanner 5. mouse 6. printer 7. headset 8. loudspeaker 9. webcam

8 Technology gets better all the time

2. The lightest laptops 3. as small/little as books 4. much nicer and quieter 5. much better monitors 6. a much more important role 7. much easier 8. more exciting than before.

9 Writing to communicate

Number two is a postcard, number three is an e-mail, number four is a diary, number five is an MSN, number six is a note, number seven is a letter and number eight is a poem.

10 Lisa writes lots of texts

2. I can't see you today. 3. Thank you for your message and picture. 4. I'll talk to you later.

11 Writing a text message

Hi Sonia. Fyi show is 2moro n costs £20. 2much, imo. Still wanna go? Tell me asap. cu, Lisa.

12 Writing notes and letters

Hi Robert, I tried to call you earlier. I have gone to the airport because Alex forgot his passport! I'll be back at ten. Would you cook dinner?/Could you cook dinner? (There is some lasagne in the freezer.) Call me if there is a problem. See you later, Maria.

13 Writing postcards

Lösungsvorschlag:
Dear Grandma and Grandpa,
We arrived safely in Paris yesterday. The weather is fantastic -really sunny and warm. The hotel is beautiful and it's right in the middle of the city. I am in a room with 3 other girls – it's bright and comfortable. Our French is a disaster but the receptionist understands us! The plan for tomorrow is the Eiffel Tower.
See you soon,
Lisa

14 Letters are not dead

2. Dear Sir or Madam, 3. I would like to know if; I am writing to ask about/if … 4. Thank you very much (for) … 5. I'm sorry about/that …; Please accept my apologies about … 6. Could you please send …; Would you be kind enough to send … 7. Please find enclosed … 8. Yours sincerely, 9. Love, 10. I look forward to hearing from you. Write soon.

15 Formal and informal letters

formal
Yours sincerely, Thank you very much for your letter. I hope to hear from you soon. Dear Mr Walker, I'm afraid I'm not satisfied with the product. Please contact us if you have any problems. I hope you like the product.
informal
Keep in touch. Lots of love, Tell me if it's not OK. Hey, it was good to hear from you.
Hello Sam, Can you send me the tickets? Enjoy!

16 Letters to customers

Lösungsvorschlag:
Dear Mr Evans,
It will be no problem to send our brochure as a pdf-file. We can deliver to the USA. Please find enclosed a list of our delivery costs in euros. Delivery takes two weeks. If you are not satisfied with the product, you can send it back to us and we will give you your money back. All you pay is postage.
We look forward to hearing from you soon.
Yours sincerely,
...

Dear Ms Lowerton,
Please accept our apologies about Greenlife. We will check this. If it has not been sent to you, we will send it immediately. We hope you will be satisfied with Greenlife.
Yours sincerely,
...

17 Could I speak to Mr White, please?

2. Who's calling please? 3. Just a moment. 4. Can you call back later? 5. Can I take a message? 6. Thank you for calling

18 Phone phrases

Mrs Best: Exeter 318795. Caroline Best speaking
Robert: Hi, its Robert here. Is Lewis at home?
Mrs Best: Sorry, Robert. Lewis is out.
Robert: Oh, do you know when he will be home?
Mrs Best: Sorry, I don't. Can I take a message?
Robert: No, it's fine. I'll call him on his mobile.
Mrs Best: Ok, Robert, I'll tell him you called.
Robert: Thanks. Goodbye.

19 First or second?

A
<u>con</u>/tact pre/<u>fer</u> <u>sur</u>/vey <u>ad</u>/vert a/<u>ddress</u> re/<u>sults</u> <u>mo</u>/bile <u>pro</u>/gramme <u>leaf</u>/let en/<u>joy</u> ex/<u>plain</u> in/<u>vent</u>

B
1. explain 2. leaflet 3. enjoy 4. invent 5. survey 6. prefer

20 Word groups

computer: Internet; keyboard; monitor; DVD; programme; software; username; webcam
telephone: caller; mobile; Pay As You Go; phone number; ring tone; text message
newspaper: advert; article; cartoon; headline; interview; journalist; reporter;
television: advert; cartoon; channel; commercial; documentary; DVD; interview; journalist; programme; reporter;

Career plans

1 The perfect job

A
1. computer engineer 2. pilot 3. beauty therapist 4. police officer

B
Lösungsvorschlag:
2. A pilot is an exciting job because you fly to different countries.
3. A cook is a stressful job because you work long hard hours.
4. A carer is a valuable job because you look after sick people.
5. A car mechanic is a useful job because cars often break down.
6. A police officer is a dangerous job because you find and arrest criminals.

2 What are our jobs?

1. dancer, actor 2. farmer, vet's assistant 3. caretaker, headteacher 4. waiter, receptionist 5. doctor, nurse 6. driver, mechanic 7. goalkeeper, tennis player 8. electrician, plumber

3 Gina

Gina works as a receptionist in a large international hotel. She usually starts work at 6 am before the guests have breakfast. She greets new guests and answers the phone. She often speaks to the guests and helps them if they have a problem. She only has 30 minutes/half an hour lunch break and she eats in the hotel. She usually goes home/leaves work at 3.30 pm. Sometimes her colleague is late and she has to stay a bit longer/later.

4 I'm good at that!

Lösungsvorschlag:
2. I'm a creative person. I enjoy travelling and seeing new places. I can imagine working for a newspaper.
3. I'm not very practical. I don't want to be my own boss. I don't think I would like to work as a plumber.

5 Strange jobs

Lösungsvorschlag:
Dog detective: If you can't find your dog and you have looked everywhere, you should ring a dog detective.
His 'colleague' – a dog – can smell and hear dogs that are far away. Together the detective and his/her dog partner will find the dog quickly and you will be happy.

6 Derek's job

2. started 3. starts; finishes 4. will start; will work 5. working; doesn't like 6. cleaning 7. saved; had fallen 8. earns; gets; works

7 'Fifteen' – a special restaurant

2. was planned 3. were offered 4. were trained 5. were taught 6. were invited 7. were cooked 8. was made; was shown 9. was built 10. were given

8 Talking about career plans

A
1. b) 2. c) 3. b) 4. a) 5. a) 6. a)

B
I'm going to do training to be a roofer when I leave school. I'm interested in different kinds of roof and later I'd like to learn about thatching (*Reetdachdecken*).

9 Advice for Maria

1. If she asks her friends, it'll be easier to talk to them. They'll know her personality and her interests. However, they won't have any real work experience. And unfortunately, they won't know what employers want or the best jobs available.
2. If she talks to her careers advisor she can find the best job because the advisor knows the best jobs that are available. But unfortunately, the advisor doesn't know Maria's skills and abilities.
3. If she talks to her parents or her relatives they have lots of experience of working life. Unfortunately, they won't know the trends in the job market.

10 A waiter's life is not an easy life

Cartoon 1 goes with C, cartoon 2 goes with A, cartoon 3 goes with D, cartoon 4 goes with B.

11 Nick's interview with a careers advisor

Nick: I've had an idea. I hope you can help me (with it).

…

Nick: I'd like to work as a DJ or a presenter for a radio station.

…

Nick: Well, I know a lot about music and I think I've got a good voice.

…

Nick: Yes, I have. Some of my friends have got a band, and I record their music. Then I sell the music online.

…

Nick: Do you know where I could do a training course, or where I could do work experience?

…

Nick: That's a good idea. I'll ring the radio station and ask them if they can help.

…

Nick: Thanks for your help. Bye/Goodbye.

12 Missing words

1. wages/salary 2. unemployed 3. tax 4. employer
5. minimum wage 6. colleagues 7. employees

13 Right person – right job

B
2. You can earn extra money as a steward/stewardess (on the cross-channel ferries) and as a waiter/waitress.
3. A secretary must have a friendly personality.
4. Gardeners and waiters/waitresses get the minimum wage.
5. Stewards on ferries and waiters/waitresses in restaurants work mostly with customers.
6. Gardeners and waiters/waitresses do the most physical work.

C
gardener
advantages: flexible hours; work outside; no experience necessary
disadvantages: work with heavy tools; hard physical work; not well-paid

steward/stewardess
advantages: good pay and bonuses; travel abroad
disadvantages: long hours; working hours not regular

secretary
advantages: regular hours; good pay
disadvantages: always work in same place; only work indoors

waiter/waitress
advantages: work in town centre so easy to get to; get big tips; work in a good team
disadvantages: only evening or weekend work; must work under pressure; only earn minimum wage

14 Working abroad

A
Lösungsvorschlag:
Man kann als Freiwillige(r) an verschiedenen Projekten in diversen Ländern arbeiten. Die Arbeitsprojekte für die Freiwilligen dauern zwischen drei und sechs Monaten. Man bewirbt sich per E-mail. Man kann, zum Beispiel, beim Bau einer Schule in Bolivien helfen; man kann Bäume pflanzen in Indien oder bei Wasserprojekten in Sudan mithelfen. Die Verpflegung und Unterkunft sind kostenlos. Den Flug muss der Freiwillige selbst zahlen, ebenso muss er Taschengeld mitbringen.

Man kann als Au Pair Mädchen oder Junge einen Sommer lang in den USA arbeiten. Man wohnt mit der Familie zusammen und betreut deren Kinder: man unterstützt sie bei den Hausaufgaben, man gestaltet ihre Freizeit mit. Die Unterkunft und den Flug zahlt die Familie. Man bekommt von der Familie auch Taschengeld. Besonders gern werden junge Männer als Au pair gesehen.

B
1. Volunteers can work for three or six months on projects.
2. Volunteers don't get a salary, they have to bring their own pocket money.
3. Volunteers can also work in South America and India.
4. Volunteers get their accommodation free.
5. Boys and girls can be au pairs. The company especially likes to employ male au pairs.
6. The au pair jobs are only for the summer.
7. The American family pays for the flight. The au pair doesn't get a salary for his/her work, but the family gives him/her pocket money.
8. The au pairs also do free time activities with the children/go out places with the children.

C
Lösungsvorschlag:
Dear Sir/Madam,
I want to help! I leave school this summer and I'd love to be a volunteer in the months before I start my job training! I think I'd be really useful for the project in Bolivia. I have often helped family and friends with renovation projects on their houses so I have a lot of experience of woodwork, painting and decorating and physical work in general. I do youth work for our church – I am the leader of a boys' free time activity group – so it would also be great if I could do something with the school children. Would that be possible?
I look forward to hearing from you soon.

15 A crossword

			1 B		2 C											3 O				
	4 S	H	O	P	A	S	S	I	5 S	T	A	N	T			F			6 C	
			S		R				I					7 F		F			R	
8 N	U	R	S	E	E		9 O		C			10 F	L	E	X	I	11 B	L	E	
E					E		U		K					R		C	O		A	
12 W	A	I	T	E	R		T				13 G			R		E	N		T	
S							S			14 E	A	R	L	Y			U		I	15 E
P			16 A	U	P	A	I	R			R					17 W	S	18 A	V	M
A	19 P						D				D					O		D	E	P
P	O		20 J	O	B	C	E	N	T	R	E				21 T	R	A	V	E	L
22 E	L	E	C	T	R	I	C	I	A	N	N					K		I		O
R	I									23 W	E	E	K	E	N	D		S		Y
	T				24 S	O	F	T	W	A	R	E				25 A	L	O	N	E
	E											26 H	E	A	V	Y		R		R

Applications and interviews

1 Applying for a job

2. read the job adverts 3. sounded perfect 4. phoned the restaurant 5. wrote a letter of application 6. invited him for an interview 7. made a good impression 8. offered him a job as a trainee cook; start on Monday

2 Writing a CV

1. motivated and reliable 2. date of birth 3. sporting achievements 4. address with postcode 5. computer skills 6. work experience 7. nationality 8. a brief summary 9. interests and hobbies 10. good qualifications 11. language skills 12. as a waiter/waitress

4 Looking for a job

1. b) 2. a) 3. c) 4. b)

5 Find the words

2. salary 3. candidates 4. headquarters 5. to expand 6. store 7. guarantee 8. customers 9. consumer electronic products (oder: consumer electronics) 10. qualifications

6 Phoning about a job

1. It's a good idea to write down all your questions before you call the company.
2. Remember the name of the person you are talking to.
3. Explain briefly why you are phoning and what you want to know.
4. It's important to make a good impression, so talk clearly and politely.
5. You don't want to forget important information, so make notes during the phone call.
6. At the end of the phone call don't forget to thank the person and say goodbye.

7 Do you have any vacancies?

1. I'd like to know if you have any vacancies at the moment.
2. Is experience (in sales/in a shop/in a store) necessary?
3. What qualifications do I need? / What qualifications should I have?
4. How can I apply? / How should I apply?
5. When could I start?
6. Can/Could you give me your address, please? / What's the company address?
7. Thank you. / Thank you very much. / Thank you for your help.

8 Julia's letter of application

A

1. I am writing to apply for …
2. Please find enclosed …
3. I have worked as a sales assistant on Saturdays.
4. Dear Mrs Davidson,
5. I look forward to hearing from you.
6. Yours sincerely,

B

Lösungsvorschlag:
Dear Sam,
I saw the advert in TeenFashion Magazine last week. I am writing to apply for the job of advertising assistant. I leave school this year and I would love to work on your magazine team.
For years I have followed fashion. At school I enjoyed working on projects about fashion and I designed the fashion pages of our monthly school magazine. At home I collect fashion photos and newspaper reports with my friends. I have had evening/Saturday jobs in clothes shops so that I could buy cool clothes. I am not afraid of hard work.
I am available for an interview at any time.
Yours sincerely,

9 Who are you?

2. advertising department 3. the receptionist 4. very busy 5. the manager 6. on holiday 7. didn't tell us 8. very helpful 9. motorbike holiday 10. Who are you? 11. completely forgotten 12. had lost my job

10 Opposites

2. started 3. indoors 4. relaxed 5. alone/on my own/with a partner 6. remembered to

11 I wouldn't employ you!

2. I think I would enjoy working as a photographer.
3. I'm sure I would have great fun and I'd meet famous people.
4. I don't want to become a plumber./I don't want to be a plumber.
5. I'm good at taking photographs.
6. I won't be lazy when I start earning money./I won't be lazy when I start to earn money.
7. They'll be more impressed when they read about my work experience.
8. The manager had forgotten to tell the others (about me). He was on holiday.
9. …

12 Two cartoons

Cartoon 1: You'll have to look harder than that to find a job, son.
Cartoon 2: I don't think much of your work experience, Eric.

13 Preparing for an interview

A

1. Make sure to wear smart, clean clothes./Remember to wear smart, clean clothes.
2. You mustn't wear your sneakers or trainers./You should never wear your sneakers or trainers.
3. Remember to go to the hairdressers./Make sure you go to the hairdressers.
4. Make sure you go to bed early the night before./Remember to go to bed early the night before.
5. Don't forget to find out where the company is./Remember to find out where the company is.
6. Make sure you get information about the company./ Remember to get information about the company./Don't forget to get information about the company.
7. Make sure you think of answers to questions they might ask you.
8. Don't forget to look at the person you are talking to./Make sure you look at the person you are talking to.
9. Don't forget to thank the person for the interview./ Remember to thank the person for the interview./Make sure you thank the person for the interview.

B

Lösungsvorschlag:
I think his father's advice is good./I think it is good advice./ I think the advice is helpful.
I don't think his father's advice is good./I don't think it is good advice./I don't think the advice is helpful.

C

Lösungsvorschlag:
Your mobile phone should not be on when you are in an interview./You should switch off your mobile when you go into the building. You can switch it on again when you leave the building.

D

2. It isn't a good idea to answer questions with 'Yes' or 'No'. Try to give the interviewer information about yourself. /Try to answer in full sentences.
3. It isn't a good idea to talk about your weaknesses. Try to talk about what you are good at.
4. It isn't a good idea to say things about yourself that are not true. Try to tell the truth.

14 Diana's interview

3. She knew nothing about the leisure centre. /She hadn't found out anything about the leisure centre.
4. She said something which wasn't true.
5. She answered the question with 'Yes'. /Her answer was too short. She didn't give the interviewer any information.
6. She didn't give a good reason why she is the right person for the job. /'Learning quickly' is not a good reason to give Diana the job. /Diana's answer had nothing to do with the skills or the qualifications you need to do the job of instructor.
7. It wasn't a good idea to tell the interviewer that she didn't like her boss.
8. Diana asked about holidays first. You should ask a question about the work first.
9. Diana didn't say she was sorry when her mobile rang. / She didn't switch off her mobile when it rang. /She hadn't switched off her mobile before she went to the interview. / You shouldn't answer your phone or send a text message during an interview.

People at work

1 Different types of work

1. 2.2 million people work in the construction industry. They do jobs such as carpenter, electrician, plumber, roofer.
2. 2 million people work in travel and tourism. They do jobs such as steward/stewardess, tour guide, receptionist, travel agent.
3. 1.3 million people work in the National Health Service. They do jobs such as carer, nurse, doctor.
4. 1.25 million people work in finance. They do jobs such as accountant and bank clerk.
5. 620,000 people work in leisure, sport and recreation. They do jobs such as coach, fitness instructor, lifeguard.
6. 250,000 people work in hairdressing and beauty. They work in jobs such as hairdresser and beauty therapist.

2 Kate Johnson

A

1. He says customers can see that I am creative.
2. wash and dry customers' hair; clean up the salon; make tea for the customers; work at reception; answer the phone; make appointments
3. I work five days a week from 10 am to 6 pm.
4. Mondays are usually free.
5. The downside of the job is that I have to stand all day. My legs really ache at the end of the day.
6. One day I would like to have my own salon and be my own boss.

B
Lösungsvorschläge:
When did you start your training?
When will you finish your training?
When is the London Hair Show?
What do you like best about your job?
What (hair) style do you like best?
What are your colleagues like?
Why did you choose this job?
Why did you choose this salon?
Where would you like to work when you have finished your training?
Where would you like to have a salon?
Would you like to work abroad after your training?

C
1. Kate works long hours to learn about cutting and colouring hair.
2. She has no time to be bored in the salon because she's always busy.
3. She meets (lots of) different people and they tell her stories about their lives and about their problems.

3 Mike Sears – a lock keeper on the river Trent

A
lock; tide; river; boat; phone; equipment; environment; summer; weekends

B
Lösungsvorschlag:
David: Did you need experience for the job?/Did you have to have experience for the job?
David: Can you open the lock gates at any time?/When can you open the lock gates?/When do you open the lock gates?
David: What else do you do?/What other jobs do you do as a lock keeper?
David: Are you lonely in your job?/Is it a lonely job?/Do you meet other people (in your job)?
David: Do you work (at) weekends, too?/Do you have to work weekends?

C
Lösungsvorschlag:
The lock keeper looks after the lock and the equipment. He/she makes sure that there is no rubbish in the river and by the lock. The lock keeper opens the lock gates for the boats at the right time – when the river is at the right level.

4 Kevin Adams – a nursery assistant

A
1. busy, hectic, loud 2. energetic, caring, patient 3. exhausted 4. curious 5. happy, proud

B
1. has been; have not stopped/haven't stopped 2. has been; have cleaned 3. have checked 4. have chosen 5. have gone

C
2. He has already practised the new song.
3. He has not written (He hasn't written) a letter to the parents yet.
4. He has not filled (He hasn't filled) the paint bottles yet.
5. He has already phoned Liam's mother.

5 Olivia Williams – a window dresser

A
1. She was good at art. She was good at making 3D models of rooms and buildings.
2. She works five days a week from 9am until 6pm.
3. She has to be flexible because at busy times of the year she has to work on Saturdays.
4. Mondays are boring. She has to tidy up the shop display after a busy Saturday.
5. When she works on a small display on her own she likes using her own ideas. She likes being creative with colours and objects.
6. The pay isn't very good. (So it helps if you love your job.)
7. Her dream is to be the display manager of the shop./She would like to be the display manager of the shop.

B
1. Olivia is polite. 2. She is flexible. 3. She is punctual. 4. She is a hard worker. 5. He can see her as a display manager.

C
Mr Denton is pleased with Olivia's work.

D
2. good at making 3. went to college 4. in a team; on her own 5. use her own ideas; be creative with colours and objects 6. walk into the window displays

E
odd word out
1. inside (Punctual, polite and creative all describe people.)
2. building (Window, door and roof are parts of a building.)
3. Saturday (Saturday is a day of the week. The others are special holiday days.)
4. qualification (School, college and university are places where you can learn.)
5. colour (Art, geography and maths are subjects at school.)
6. calendar (Week, year, month are parts of a calendar.)

6 Starting your own business

A
2. borrowed 3. had no idea; called 4. organised; gave 5. sold 6. ate; became 7. had opened 8. bought

B
Lösungsvorschlag:
I'd like to start my own business. I think I'd be a good manager. I'm good at organising things. I would open a bicycle shop with a bicycle repair service. I'm good at repairing bikes. And I'm polite and friendly with people. People always have problems with bikes. Most people have no time to repair their bike themselves.

7 Say it in English

2. What do you like best about your job?
3. My friend Ina is unemployed.
4. I'm looking for a new job.
5. What qualifications do I need for the job?/What qualifications do I have to have for the job?

8 Tools and equipment for the job

A
1. camera 2. comb 3. desk 4. laptop 5. hammer 6. spanner 7. chainsaw 8. frying pan 9. ladder 10. oil 11. screwdriver 12. scisscors 13. phone 14. spade 15. knife

B

2. carpenter: screwdriver; hammer
3. gardener: spade; chainsaw
4. cook: frying pan; knife
5. receptionist: phone; desk
6. mechanic: oil; spanner
7. fireman: hosepipe; ladder
8. hairdresser: scissors; comb

9 What are they used for?

2. Scissors are used for cutting hair.
3. A camera is used for taking photos.
4. A frying pan is used for cooking food.
5. A spanner is used for repairing engines.
6. A chainsaw is used for cutting down trees.
7. A hammer is used for hitting nails into wood.
8. A spade is used for digging in the garden.

10 Safety at work

A

The person in photo A is wearing a hard hat and goggles.
The person in photo B is wearing a face shield, gloves and overalls.
The person in photo C is wearing a hard hat, an ear muff, boots and gloves.

B

2. You wear an ear muff to protect your ears.
3. You wear gloves to protect your hands.
4. You wear goggles to protect your eyes.
5. You wear a face shield to protect your face.
6. You wear boots to protect your feet.
7. You wear overalls to protect your normal clothes.

11 Signs

A

1. You must wear a hard hat. 2. You mustn't go in here. 3. You must wear goggles, an ear muff and boots. 4. You can use this to put out a small fire. 5. No mobiles! 6. You can stop a machine with this button.

B

1. This is where you leave the building if there is a fire or other problem.
2. This is where you can find all the things you need if you have an accident. /This is where you get help if you have an accident or if you are ill at work.